Critical Storytelling in Unc

CONSTRUCTING KNOWLEDGE: CURRICULUM STUDIES IN ACTION

Volume 9

Scope

"Curriculum" is an expansive term; it encompasses vast aspects of teaching and learning. Curriculum can be defined as broadly as, "The content of schooling in all its forms" (English, p. 4), and as narrowly as a lesson plan. Complicating matters is the fact that curricula are often organized to fit particular time frames. The incompatible and overlapping notions that curriculum involves everything that is taught and learned in a particular setting *and* that this learning occurs in a limited time frame reveal the nuanced complexities of curriculum studies.

"Constructing Knowledge" provides a forum for systematic reflection on the substance (subject matter, courses, programs of study), purposes, and practices used for bringing about learning in educational settings. Of concern are such fundamental issues as: What should be studied? Why? By whom? In what ways? And in what settings? Reflection upon such issues involves an inter-play among the major components of education: subject matter, learning, teaching, and the larger social, political, and economic contexts, as well as the immediate instructional situation. Historical and autobiographical analyses are central in understanding the contemporary realties of schooling and envisioning how to (re)shape schools to meet the intellectual and social needs of all societal members. Curriculum is a social construction that results from a set of decisions; it is written and enacted and both facets undergo constant change as contexts evolve.

This series aims to extend the professional conversation about curriculum in contemporary educational settings. Curriculum is a designed experience intended to promote learning. Because it is socially constructed, curriculum is subject to all the pressures and complications of the diverse communities that comprise schools and other social contexts in which citizens gain self-understanding.

Critical Storytelling in Uncritical Times

Stories Disclosed in a Cultural Foundations of Education Course

Edited by

Nicholas D. Hartlep and Brandon O. Hensley
Illinois State University, USA

SENSE PUBLISHERS
ROTTERDAM/BOSTON/TAIPEI

A C.I.P. record for this book is available from the Library of Congress.

ISBN: 978-94-6300-254-7 (paperback)
ISBN: 978-94-6300-255-4 (hardback)
ISBN: 978-94-6300-256-1 (e-book)

Published by: Sense Publishers,
P.O. Box 21858,
3001 AW Rotterdam,
The Netherlands
https://www.sensepublishers.com/

All chapters in this book have undergone peer review.

Cover design by Tak Toyoshima

Printed on acid-free paper

For my wife Stacey Elise Hartlep

You're my Florence Nightingale.
Thank you for the endless support.

For my wife Melissa and my family

Especially my grandpa, who didn't make it to see this book,
and my grandma, who always supported my educational journey.

Activist scholars Hartlep and Hensley challenge readers to rethink good teaching by providing readers with rich, authentic narratives that were co-produced by students in a Cultural Foundations of Education Course. *Critical Storytelling in Uncritical Times* is a thoughtfully conceived communal writing project and a significant milestone in our mutual struggle for liberation and human dignity.
Suzanne SooHoo, Ph.D., Hassinger Chair in Education and Co-Director, Paulo Freire Democratic Project, Chapman University

In this invigorating and wide-ranging volume, Nicholas D. Hartlep and Brandon O. Hensley work with a group of courageous doctoral students in a Cultural Foundations of Education class to reflect on their backgrounds, experiences, and personal and professional interests and critically examine the ways in which their personal histories, languages, cultures, identities, and experiences affect who they are, how they interact with others, and how they live out "major concepts," "big ideas," and "general principles" of teaching and learning in life and inquiry. Their gripping stories and critical reflections invent counternarratives that extend understandings of their stories and stories of others regarding experiences of migration, displacement, slavery, suppression, repression, resistance, representation, difference, spirituality, race, gender, place, and responses to racism, sexism, classism, heterosexism, ageism, ableism, and other forms of oppression. Their counternarratives, as theories and methods, expose unjust and dehumanizing ideas, policies, and practices, contextualize silenced and unexamined narratives of their experiences and experiences of underrepresented or disenfranchised individuals and groups, raise challenging questions, protest against the supremacy and normality of meta or official narratives, and transgress orthodoxy and dogma epistemologically and methodologically. This publication advances the field by exemplifying critical story telling to honor practical, contextual, and theoretical diversities, contradictions, and complexities, and to invent pedagogical possibilities to cultivate a more balanced and equitable human condition that embodies cultural, linguistic, sociopolitical, and ecological diversity and plurality of individuals, groups, tribes, and societies in a contested and unjust world.

Ming Fang He, Ph.D., Professor of Curriculum Studies, Georgia Southern University

Through stories, we construct the past, compose the present, and imagine the future. As contemporary educational policies promote standardization through empirical data, the significance of telling and listening to one another's narratives through critical lenses becomes increasingly imperative. In this book, Hartlep and Hensley highlight the *why* and *how* of critical storytelling in the crucial context of a cultural foundations classroom. Framed by Haberman's tenets of good teaching, the process of collective composition is both innovative and deeply resonant. Each chapter illustrates a perspective of education that traces a personal past in ways that challenge us to envision new collective possibilities. Taken together, the components of this groundbreaking text offer a riveting read for teachers, teacher educators, and anyone interested in seeking justice through transformative teaching and learning.

Julie Gorlewski, Ph.D., Associate Professor, State University of New York at New Paltz, Editor, **English Journal**

TABLE OF CONTENTS

DEREK M. BOLEN

FOREWORD

CRITICAL STORIES, CRITICAL IMAGINATIONS, AND CRITICAL POSSIBILITIES

The places we stand in the academy are markedly important—not just in the pragmatic ways that they position us to move ahead, fall behind, become credentialed, or usher us toward the exit of our careers, but in the ways that they position us to reach outside of the academy and into the lives of others. Where we stand, where we find ourselves located, it isn't just happenstance. At least, for good reason, it ought not to be. In the performance and struggle of scholar/teacher, teacher/scholar, we spend much time getting our footing. Sometimes it's on the brink of Pavlovian; other times it's steeped in something like Michel de Certeau's (1984) strategies and tactics. As quickly as Paulo Freire (e.g., Freire 1970, 2000; Freire, Freire, & Oliveira, 2014) may free us, our advisors or chairs or deans or senior scholars at conferences make clear the disparity of where our feet are and where they need to be. Yet, somehow, if we're tenacious, we find our footing—never alone, never without the relation to/with others.

* * *

This last day of class marks what will likely be the last time that I teach gender and communication before I finish my Ph.D. It's a course that's found its way into my heart and—at the risk of sounding sappy—my soul. Walking into our classroom, I see 20 students in a circle—one they've built with trust and purpose. I don't know exactly what I'll say this last day of class, but that's not uncommon. After coming to our class for the past 15 weeks to teach them, to learn from them, to learn for them, I am both happy and sad that our critical interpretive expedition into an ocean of gender, sexuality, and communication is coming to an end. I am happy for the discussions, the critical interrogations of normativity, the getting-to-know-yous, and the relationships. I am sad for the impending goodbyes. To express their growth and ability to critically think about that which we so often take for granted, they chose to write their final project as autoethnographies. Reading autoethnographies in class alongside critical, interpretive, and yes, even a little post-positivist work, created space in the classroom for each of us to live with the stories of others (Frank, 1995). After a few minutes of chat, we ready ourselves to hear each other's stories. Only sharing if you want. And only sharing what you want.

She reads from her paper first. She's a dance instructor and full-time college student. Her thoughtful contributions to class discussion often critiqued the practices of teaching children's dance classes, but as she begins it becomes clear that she's held back. She stories everyday trauma of growing up in dance. In a shift to dialogue that has been integrated into her narrative, she reaccounts communication where by the time she was seven she had been called fat and forced to diet by eight. As she eloquently and evocatively shows her story, her steady hand presents a photo of her 7-year-old self for us to see. I see a young girl, thin by normative standards. The story is juxtaposed with experiences she has had instructing dance, years later. Experiences through which she has, now as an instructor, come uncomfortably close to her own childhood experiences. As she shifts back to storying her childhood, her eyes well up with tears. Listening, watching, thinking, and feeling—I am aware that my eyes have welled up with tears too. I vow to not look away—not with my eyes, nor my mind, nor my heart. I vow to give her my support, making myself vulnerable by being there with her. But I look away for only a second to see the rest of the class, their faces—foreheads, eyes, mouths—just as I imagine my own. I imagine their hearts and minds the same way. In the seconds that it has taken for this aesthetic moment (Bolen, 2014) to be shared, she has empowered herself to continue telling her story.

She concludes her story, and the class claps. The applause sounds and feels like something more than what I am used to after speeches in Public Speaking. We sit quietly, but only for a bit before her classmates begin complimenting her. After the compliments subside, a short discussion begins about many of the critical ideas that we have been working with all semester. Her narrative also creates a space for and offers an invitation for the narratives of others, which intersect her storied experience in a multitude of ways. We continue paper-by-paper, not all evocative in the same way as hers, but all evocative and invitational in their own ways. At the conclusion of the final discussion—when it takes everything in me not to cry—I move to the hallway while they complete their end of the semester student evaluations of the course.

In an empty hallway and alone, I think about the stories that have just been shared with our class. These weren't simply stories written, shown, and shared for grades. These were self-liberatory stories. Stories in which students staked claims in the personal and political; these were stories that purposefully engaged their vulnerability—once in writing, and once more in sharing and showing. This was a collaborative undertaking whereby students embraced the fact that it was with and through each other that this segment of their stories' voyages would find a temporary port. I momentarily ponder their trust in me, but then crumble in awe of their trust in each other, in their selves. I didn't do this. We did this. Together.

They start coming out into the hallway one at a time. Each person says something about this class, how I have helped them grow to see the world in new ways. Before they hug me goodbye, I do my best to tell them how this class—how *they* have helped me to grow and see the world in new ways. After the last student walks away, I dash to the stairwell for the cathartic cry that I've been yearning for since class began.

When I look back, now more than three years later, I am still in awe of the way that we learned together, from each other, from me. Or, perhaps more accurately, the way that we couldn't have learned without each other. I think it's for collaborative moments like this that I am a teacher. And even if it takes another six years of teaching to be in this moment again—I am hooked. Because it reminds me what I meant when I said that I loved to teach. It reminds me what it means, what it's like when the classroom isn't wielded as a site of indoctrination, but instead as a space for collaborative liberation.

* * *

On the cusp of beginning my tenth year teaching at the university-level, I'm teaching a summer graduate seminar on teaching communication in higher education. Our graduate seminar room is like most others. There's a rectangular table, and students sit on either of the long sides. The teacher sits at one of the heads. This will be the second time that I teach this class, but this time around marks the ninth anniversary since I took the class over 1,400 miles away as a student. Some things have changed since I was a student in this class. For instance, I can't fit into the same t-shirts, I am allowed to get married in more than one state, I have a dog (Raider), I fell in love with teaching, and now I sit at the head of the table. The very head of the table that we'll go on to critique as we read Deanna Fassett and John Warren's (2007) *Critical Communication Pedagogy*. Some things have stayed the same— most notably, the importance of storytelling in this classroom space. Fassett and Warren called for teachers to tell their stories in a bid for reflexivity and a critical move toward making the classroom (and the world) a more socially just place. We tell stories for a number of reasons, but in the classroom I believe it has something to do with Art Bochner's (1994, 2002) observation that our stories are our theories of life based on personal experience. When teachers tell soon-to-be teachers stories of their time in the classroom, students have the potential to pick up some "equipment for living" (Burke, 1974, p. 293) as teachers in the classroom. When students tell stories of their personal experiences, they may impart possibility upon other students and teachers.

Telling personal stories does not come without risk. Then again, there's also a certain amount of risk in not telling personal stories. For the longest time, we weren't allowed to tell personal stories in social scientific inquiry (*cf.* Denzin & Lincoln, 2011). As the genres of social science and humanities began to blur (Geertz, 1983), fields of possibility opened for including personal narrative into our inquiry. A number of methods, going by innumerable names, were eventually framed under the moniker *autoethnography* (*cf.* Ellis & Bochner, 2000). The definitions for autoethnography are too numerous to recount here, so I will say this: autoethnography is the reflexive process of looking to the past to make sense of the present with a hopeful eye on the future for the sake of self, relationship, other, culture, and society. Imaginings and articulations of autoethnography have (re)framed it as, among other things, interpretive (*cf.* Denzin, 2014), performative (*cf.* Spry, 2011), and critical (*cf.* Boylorn & Orbe, 2014a).

It's humbling to tell the story that comes—in terms of the order of pages comprising this book—before the stories of others. Then again, there are a myriad of stories that came before any of my own (including, if not especially, before this one)—stories that are not bound in this book, yet are inextricably interwoven into it. These are the stories that make our stories possible in both personal and political ways—as teachers and students, scholars and practitioners, and selves and others.

What Hartlep, Hensley, and the rest of the storytellers in this book accomplish is reflexively locating and relocating their places, their footings, and reaching outward in hope. In a critical storytelling undertaking, such as this current edited collection, I am reminded of Robin Boylorn and Mark Orbe's (2014b) words on doing critical autoethnography: "We write as an Other, and for an Other" (p. 15). When our autoethnographies encapsulate this sentiment, we have the potential to tell critical stories, engage critical imaginations, and craft critical possibilities.

REFERENCES

Bochner, A. P. (1994). Perspectives on inquiry II: Theories and stories. In M. L. Knapp & G. R. Miller (Eds.), *Handbook of interpersonal communication* (2nd ed., pp. 21–41). Thousand Oaks, CA: Sage.

Bochner, A. P. (2002). Perspectives on inquiry III: The moral of stories. In M. L. Knapp & J. A. Daly (Eds.), *Handbook of interpersonal communication* (3rd ed., pp. 73–101). Thousand Oaks, CA: Sage.

Bolen, D. M. (2014). After dinners, in the garage, out of doors, and climbing on rocks: Writing aesthetic moments of father-son. In J. Wyatt & T. E. Adams (Eds.), *On (writing) families: Autoethnographies of presence and absence, love and loss* (pp. 141–148). Rotterdam, The Netherlands: Sense Publishers.

Boylorn, R. M., & Orbe, M. P. (Eds.). (2014a). *Critical autoethnography: Intersecting cultural identities in everyday life*. Walnut Creek, CA: Left Coast Press.

Boylorn, R. M., & Orbe, M. P. (2014b). Introduction: Critical autoethnography as method of choice. In R. M. Boylorn & M. P. Orbe (Eds.), *Critical autoethnography: Intersecting cultural identities in everyday life* (pp. 13–26). Walnut Creek, CA: Left Coast Press.

Burke, K. (1974). *The philosophy of literary form: Studies in symbolic action* (3rd ed.). Berkeley, CA: University of California Press.

de Certeau, M. (1984). *The practice of everyday life* (S. Rendall, Trans.). Berkeley, CA: University of California Press. (Original work published 1980)

Denzin, N. K. (2014). *Interpretive autoethnography* (2nd ed.). Thousand Oaks, CA: Sage.

Denzin, N. K., & Lincoln, Y. S. (2011). Introduction: The discipline and practice of qualitative research. In N. K. Denzin & Y. S. Lincoln (Eds.), *The Sage handbook of qualitative research* (4th ed., pp. 1–20). Thousand Oaks, CA: Sage.

Ellis, C., & Bochner, A. P. (2000). Autoethnography, personal narrative, reflexivity: Researcher as subject. In N. K. Denzin & Y. S. Lincoln (Eds.), *Handbook of qualitative research* (2nd ed., pp. 773–768). Thousand Oaks, CA: Sage.

Fassett, D. L., & Warren, J. W. (2007). *Critical communication pedagogy.* Thousand Oaks, CA: Sage.

Frank, A. W. (1995). *The wounded storyteller*. Chicago, IL: University of Chicago Press.

Freire, P. (1970). *Pedagogy of the oppressed*. New York, NY: Continuum.

Freire, P. (2000). *Pedagogy of freedom: Ethics, democracy and civic courage*. New York, NY: Lanham, Rowman & Littlefield.

Freire, P., Freire, A. M. A., & Oliveira, W. F. (2014). *Pedagogy of solidarity*. Walnut Creek, CA: Left Coast Press.

Geertz, C. (1983). *Local knowledge: Further essays in interpretive anthropology*. New York, NY: Basic Books.

Spry, T. (2011). *Body, paper, stage: Writing and performing autoethnography*. Walnut Creek, CA: Left Coast Press.

PREFACE

The idea for writing a book as a class was born in a doctoral-level Cultural Foundations of Education course I taught during the summer of 2014. Initially, uncertainty permeated the course, especially during the first day when I informed the class that we would collaboratively write the syllabus for the course. The class was composed of doctoral students with a wide range of backgrounds, experiences, and professional interests. Second-year students shared the space with those who were nearing their comprehensive examinations. We had various disciplines represented as well, such as School Psychology, Communication Studies, and Higher Education. Some students had previously published book chapters and/or articles, while others had not yet published anything. These dynamics caused students to be pulled outside of their comfort zones. However, over time, our uncertainty and anxiety dissipated and transformed individuals into a community of learners. One of the course's many strengths was the collaborative spirit that stitched it, and the book that stands before the reader, together.

I must also be honest: I did not know what to expect. I knew I wanted to do a project like this book, but I was uncertain that students would buy into it and want to participate. In class, I spoke a lot about transformation and transparency. To me, transparency is incredibly important whenever "social justice" work is being done, or said to be. By asking students to do such a project, I felt vulnerable, since the perception could be that I was a predator, eager to publish off the backs of my students. This was not the case. I informed students that I wanted to create knowledge with them and make memories. The process of writing (and editing) a book with students is memorable, and the physical book is a manifestation of knowledge that we produced together.

As the instructor of the Cultural Foundations of Education course, I served as the book's primary editor. Every student but two served as a chapter contributor, and one (Brandon Hensley) served as second editor. We worked together inside and outside of class and gave substantive feedback on each person's chapter. When reviewing each other's work, we were careful to express an "ethic of care"—we acknowledged that writing is a personal and deeply political process. The class took on an almost workshop-style environment, since the course met Mondays and Wednesdays from 1:00–4:00 p.m. The volume that stands before the reader is a co-constructed collaboration, and contains a breadth of perspectives on issues of importance and relevance to a Cultural Foundations of Education course.

From the first day of class—when we worked on the course syllabus together—to the end when the book was completed, everything we have done was collaborative and driven by consensus. The syllabus and the process of this edited book project centered on Martin Haberman's (2004, pp. 54–57) 11 indicators of good teaching:

1. Whenever *students are involved with issues they regard as vital concerns*, good teaching is going on;

2. Whenever *students are involved with explanations of human differences*, good teaching is going on;

3. Whenever *students are being helped to see major concepts, big ideas, and general principles* and not merely engaged in the pursuit of isolated facts, good teaching is going on;

4. Whenever *students are involved in planning what they will be doing*, it is likely that good teaching is going on;

5. Whenever *students are involved with applying ideals such as fairness, equity, or justice to their world*, it is likely good teaching is going on;

6. Whenever *students are directly involved in real-life experience*, it is likely that good teaching is going on;

7. Whenever *students are actively involved in heterogeneous groups*, it is likely that good teaching is going on;

8. Whenever *students are asked to think about an idea in a way that questions common sense or an assumption accepted as "good" by everyone, or relates new ideas to ones learned previously, or applies an idea to the problems of living*, good teaching is going on;

9. Whenever *students are involved in redoing, re-polishing or perfecting their work*, it is likely good teaching is going on;

10. Whenever *teachers involve students with technology of information access*, good teaching is going on; and

11. Whenever *students are involved in reflecting upon their own lives and how they have come to believe and feel as they do*, good teaching is going on.

In breaking down each of Haberman's indicators of good teaching, we can unpack how they played out during this collaborative reading, writing, and learning endeavor.

1. Students Are Involved with Issues They Regard as Vital Concerns

Each student selected articles to discuss that interested him or her professionally and/or personally. In addition to self-selection of readings, students chose what story they would tell in their chapter. The breadth of writing styles, approaches to inquiry, authorial rituals, and interpretive frames spoke to the diverse disciplinary backgrounds of everyone in the room as well as to the stories we found meaningful in our lives. Writing bounced back and forth from Microsoft Word to a shared Google document where chats routinely happened outside of "class time," and the hard work of revising, critiquing, and rewriting flourished amid a constructively supportive culture; practicing an "ethic of care" became the norm—in a six-week summer class, no less.

2. Students Are Involved with Explanations of Human Differences

Many of the chapters address human differences. Our discussions, both in class and online, grappled with difference and the difference it can make—especially considering the insidious power of whiteness to name, divide, and conquer. Students and professor alike shared difficult experiences with racism, bullying, being made to feel different (or "like nothing," as one student put it), and other lived turning points, as well as times when privilege was maintained through complicity or perpetuated intentionally for one's own advantage.

Together, we unmasked "taken-for-granted" privilege vulnerably and reflexively, exploring our experiences and ourselves as sites of *difference* and *resistance*. In the spaces of the classroom and the Google document, we worked toward a deeper understanding of Warren's (2008) words: "Difference need not be coded in the negative, as an opposition (i.e., I'm different than you), but could be seen as an affirmation (i.e., I'm unique and so are you)... [D]ifference is the inevitable thread that makes us who we are and can be a beautiful thing" (p. 295).

3. *Students Are Being Helped to See Major Concepts, Big Ideas, and General Principles*

The students stretched their vocabularies to embrace disciplines that were new to many of them, and as a class we explored epistemologies that challenge the prevailing post-positivist research paradigm. Our ways of knowing were enhanced by the texts we read as a class, works that challenge hegemony as well as perpetuations and reifications of whiteness, neoliberalism, stereotypes, and oppression in various forms (Accapadi, 2007; Beadie, 1996; Becker, 1972; Carlson, 2008; Hayes & Hartlep, 2013; Hodsown & Busseri, 2012; Neuman, 2010; Norton & Sommers, 2011; Peterson & Davila, 2011; Winkle-Wagner, 2010).

4. *Students Are Involved in Planning What They Will Be Doing*

This book was planned, written, and edited by course participants. The stories shared in each chapter were completely at the discretion of the author. In this sense, participants were given complete agency to voice their narrative, to investigate what stories matter to them. The choice to publish final chapters was left to the authors, whether they published in the book or elsewhere (Editors' note: As mentioned previously, two students elected not to publish their story).

5. *Students Are Involved with Applying Ideals such as Fairness, Equity, and Justice to their World*

Course participants spent significant time discussing the previously referenced readings and brought additional articles to the group in class and online. Our readings and conversations revealed vulnerable experiences, struggles with the depths of hegemony and complicity, but also included turning points and optimism. We worked to critically read our lives and tell our stories through a process that "embraces fluidity, resists definitional and conceptual fixity, looks to self and structures as relational accomplishments, and takes seriously the needs to create more livable, equitable, and just ways of living" (Adams & Holman-Jones, 2008, p. 384).

6. *Students Are Directly Involved in Real-Life Experiences*

In this collaborative volume, students were directly involved in a real-life experience of the publishing world—a world that very much thrives on maintaining whiteness, hierarchy, and the "old guard" of the academy. We worked under a hard deadline, using the final meetings for extensive editing sessions. Some students were anxious about having a publish-ready piece by the time the course ended, but the group worked extremely well under these conditions—both during meeting times and remotely. Treating one another as colleagues, we discussed the political reality in which academic publishing is situated: How editorial boards and the "blind" peer-review process serve dominant epistemologies and whiteness. The group considered different titles (all generated by the students), weighed prospective publishers, and negotiated ways of ordering chapters, among other authorial decisions. On the final day of class, we did the work of filling out copyright release forms and finalizing last details. All told, it was a remarkable real-life experience.

7. Students Are Actively Involved in Heterogeneous Groups

Students wrote in heterogeneous groups. The abilities and prior experiences ranged greatly, but this was an asset rather than a limitation. Those with a wealth of experience in writing and publishing were able to mentor those who were new to it. Readers with contrasting backgrounds and experiences were able to challenge writers and clarify their prose. Heterogeneity was what made the course and producing this book both enlivening and enlightening.

8. Students Are Asked to Think about an Idea in a Way that Questions Common Sense or an Assumption Accepted as "Good" by Everyone, or Relate New Ideas to Ones Learned Previously, or Apply an Idea to the Problems of Living

While working on this book, students discussed myriad sociocultural issues. In particular, one that stood out to me was how "whiteness" (Hayes & Hartlep, 2013) is perpetuated through supposedly fair and objective conventions of scholarly writing, such as the *APA Manual* (Thompson, 2004). Although I was intimately familiar with the writings of Audrey Thompson, a student brought her essay "Gentlemanly Orthodoxy: Critical Race Feminism, Whiteness Theory, and the *APA Manual*" to my attention—which left me asking myself, "How on earth have I never read this before?" This experience speaks to how professors are always learning from their students. Professors who say or believe otherwise are deluding themselves.

9. Students Are Involved in Redoing, Polishing, and Perfecting their Work

The final chapters were rewritten and polished a dizzying number of times. A testament to our diligence, it was remarkable we pulled off writing this book in a 6-week summer course. All chapter contributors were invited to comment on the chapters of every other author, co-creating a finished product that surpasses the ability of any one author or two editors.

10. Teachers Involve Students with Technology of Information Access

This book was written and edited using Google documents. This allowed course participants to interact synchronously or asynchronously. It also enabled us to read each other's most recent materials. As opposed to writing a document in Microsoft Word and emailing it back and forth with track-changes, Google facilitated document sharing—we also uploaded readings to a Google.drive folder—and we were able to write our chapters directly into the document. As the professor of this course, I have used Google documents quite a bit. Many of the students had never used this technology before; consequently, it was a positive experience, even if it tested the patience of a few.

11. Students Are Involved in Reflecting Upon their Own Lives and How They Have Come to Believe and Feel as They Do

Often the stories told herein emanated from lived experience. These stories allowed authors to reflect upon their own lives and how they have come to believe and feel as they do. As Ellis (2004) writes, "The stories we write provide a snapshot that holds us in place for others—and ourselves—to interpret from multiple points of views, locations, and times" (p. 343). Reflection of what we believe to be true is significant, and was a significant part of this Cultural Foundations of Education course.

THE STUDENT AND HIS OR HER STORY AS CURRICULUM

The Cultural Foundations of Education course curriculum was everyone's lived experiences, enacted in discussions, and constituted in the publication of this volume. Each and every day we reworked our writing as well as our thinking. I learned a tremendous amount from the students; I hope they likewise took something valuable away from the course. At the very least, I hope I succeeded in my intention to be transparent and vulnerable.

In chapter one, "Letter to a Rural White," Jamie Neville aims to reveal a more complex and nuanced understanding of privilege and whiteness to the reader. Its intended audience is any self-professed "colorblind" rural white, including the author at age 16. He includes a remedial introduction to whiteness, and challenges the reader to recognize culturally sheltered origins and unexamined assumptions.

In chapter two, "Karma Doesn't Have to Be a Bitch: Justice-Oriented Lessons I Learned Through Death and Introspection," Nicholas Hartlep shares his personal experience of being bullied in high school and his thoughts when one of the bullies died 12 years later. Drawing on Banks and Banks' (1998) suggestion of using "fiction" to ground his chapter, Hartlep envisions what might transpire if Tom (a pseudonym), after he died, became his Cultural Foundations of Education graduate student. Hartlep shares justice-oriented lessons he learned by analyzing the death of his high school bully, Tom, through introspection.

In chapter three, "'Micro(act)gressions': Real Lessons Learned from Fake Dialogue," Amanda Rohan reflects on her experience delivering racial microaggressions to Black female college students and utilizing deception during an on-campus research study. Rohan also reflects on her life as a White female growing up in the South and how these experiences, when combined with her recent involvement conducting research on racial microaggressions, have influenced her personal and professional development in terms of her worldview as a future school psychologist.

In chapter four, "'Mis-Education': Why Teachers Need Foundations of Education Courses," Kathleen O'Brien shares the story of attending a racialized production of *Snow White* as a first-grade teacher, and considers how her K–12 experiences have culminated in her desire to teach Social Foundations of Education to pre-service teachers. Drawing on sociocultural and constructivist approaches, she discusses the importance and relevance Social Foundations of Education courses have for preparing pre-service teachers.

In chapter five, "Overcoming Cultural Barriers: Reflection of a Saudi Arabian International Student in the United States," Saad Alahmari explores his experience as an international student in the U.S. He reflects on his work and schooling in Saudi Arabia, the systems of education he has encountered in both countries, and his goals to help others overcome cultural barriers. In his story, Alahmari stresses the importance of an informal culture in the classroom where serious discussions can be raised and where learning is approached openly.

In chapter six, "Judging Stories: Narrative Value in Scholarships," Christopher Downing shares how the stories required in community college scholarship applications are judged and evaluated outside of the person telling them, and what such actions can mean to the student and the institution.

In chapter seven, "One Unheard Voice from the Shadows," Cyndy Alvarez shares a letter describing the challenges a U.S. student whose parents are undocumented encounters. Alvarez, as a school psychologist in training, reflects on this student's (Emma's) experience. Emma's letter provides one unheard voice from the shadows—one voice of 5.5 million children with undocumented parents residing in the United States.

In chapter eight, "Academic Hazing: A Reflection of My First Year Teaching at a Predominantly White Institution," Tuwana Wingfield reflects on her experiences teaching Social Work at a Predominantly White Institution (PWI). She argues that research is needed to address the preparation of White students who work with populations that have been historically marginalized and disenfranchised. From a Black feminist lens, Wingfield contends that White students experience cognitive dissonance when confronted with their own distorted images of African Americans, especially women. Through the use of "life notes," Wingfield shares her unique experiences, lessons learned, and strategies to overcome what she terms "teaching while Black." This chapter holds implications for social work education, policy, practice, and recruitment.

In chapter nine, "We are not 'Cordwood': Critical Stories and the Two-Tier System in U.S. Higher Education," Brandon Hensley explores systemic inequities in academe. He stories his experience in a departmental faculty meeting where students were compared to cheap firewood and adjunct faculty were informed their jobs were safe for another semester. Using an autoethnographic method, Hensley weaves together fragments of personal narrative, conversations with faculty, and emerging literature on contingent faculty working conditions. Utilizing a Freirean lens in problematizing dominant discourses and banking narratives in higher education, vestiges of faculty oppression are found in false charity statements such as "we appreciate all your hard work" and other benevolent communicative acts. Hensley echoes Denzin and Giardina's (2014) call for qualitative inquiry outside the academy, arguing for the necessity of stories across multimedia to aid in resistance to what Giroux (2014) calls neoliberalism's war on higher education in America.

In chapter ten, "Mr. Dolce Gabbana," Michael Cermak recounts his time as principal of New Deal High School (a pseudonym). Years later, he found out that one of his students named him Mr. Dolce Gabbana because of the small "D & G" insignia on the side of his glasses. Despite different backgrounds, Cermak and his students were able to overcome mistrust. Cermak also reflects on how he came to realize his place of privilege.

In chapter eleven, "Tapping a Dry Well: A Closer Look at Rural Education Philanthropy," Erik Dalmasso begins by reflecting on the irony he experienced while attending an enrollment management conference at an elite private university. He documents literature detailing how elite institutions and rural institutions of higher learning approach philanthropic practices. Drawing upon lessons learned from the conference—as well as diverse theoretical lenses regarding philanthropic mechanisms in non-profit settings—Dalmasso stresses the need for greater awareness of gaps in rural education funding and for additional scholarship that enables students from rural settings to access higher education.

REFERENCES

Accapadi, M. M. (2007). When white women cry: How white women's tears oppress women of color. *College Student Affairs Journal, 26*(2), 208–215.

Adams, T. E., & Holman Jones, S. (2008). Autoethnography is queer. In N. K. Denzin, Y. S. Lincoln, & L. T. Smith (Eds.), *Handbook of critical and indigenous methodologies* (pp. 373–390). Thousand Oaks, CA: Sage.

Banks, A., & Banks, S. P. (Eds.). (1998). *Fiction & social research: By ice or fire.* Walnut Creek, CA: AltaMira.

Beadie, N. (1996). From "teacher as decision maker" to teacher as participant in "shared decision making": Reframing the purpose of social foundations of education. *Teachers College Record, 98*(1), 77–103.

Becker, H. S. (1972). A school is a lousy place to learn anything in. *American Behavioral Scientist, 16*(1), 85–105. Retrieved from http://dx.doi.org/10.1177/000276427201600109

Carlson, D. (2008). Conflict of the faculties: Democratic progressivism in the age of "No child left behind." *Educational Studies, 43*(2), 94–113. Retrieved from http://dx.doi.org/10.1080/00131940801944488

Denzin, N. K., & Giardina, M. D. (Eds.). (2014). *Qualitative inquiry outside the academy.* Walnut Creek, CA: Left Coast Press.

Ellis, C. (2004). *The ethnographic I: A methodological novel about autoethnography.* WalnutCreek, CA: AltaMira Press.

Giroux, H. (2014). *Neoliberalism's war on higher education.* Chicago, IL: Haymarket Books.

Haberman, M. (2004). *Star teachers: The ideology and best practices of effective teachers of children and youth in poverty.* Houston, TX: The Haberman Educational Foundation.

Hayes, C., & Hartlep, N. (Eds.). (2013). *Unhooking from whiteness: The key to dismantling racism in the United States.* Rotterdam, The Netherlands: Sense Publishers. Retrieved from http://dx.doi.org/10.1007/978-94-6209-377-5

Hodsown, G., & Busseri, M. A. (2012). Bright minds and dark attitudes: Lower cognitive ability predicts greater prejudice through right-wing ideology and low intergroup contact. *Psychological Science, 23*(2), 187–195. Retrieved from http://dx.doi.org/10.1177/0956797611421206

Neumann, R. (2010). Social foundations and multicultural education course requirements in teacher preparation programs in the United States. *Educational Foundations, 24*(3/4), 3–17.

Norton, M., & Sommers, S. (2011). Whites see racism as a zero-sum game that they are now losing. *Perspectives on Psychological Science, 6*(3), 215–218. Retrieved from http://dx.doi.org/10.1177/1745691611406922

Peterson, R. R., & Davila, E. R. (2011). Are the walls of injustice tumbling down? *Educational Foundations, 25*(3–4), 37–58.

Thompson, A. (2004). Gentlemanly orthodoxy: Critical race feminism, whiteness theory, and the APA manual. *Educational Theory, 54*(1), 27–57. Retrieved from http://dx.doi.org/10.1111/j.1741-5446.2004.t01-5-00abs.x

Warren, J. T. (2008). Performing difference: Repetition in context. *Journal of International and Intercultural Communication, 1*(4), 290–308. Retrieved from http://dx.doi.org/10.1080/17513050802344654

Winkle-Wagner, R. (2010). Foundations of educational inequality: Cultural capital and social reproduction. *ASHE Higher Education Report, 36*(1), 1–21. Retrieved from http://dx.doi.org/10.1002/aehe.3601

JAMIE NEVILLE

1. LETTER TO A RURAL WHITE

Are you racist? No? Good, then this letter is to you.

I am a 29-year-old white male from a primarily rural background.[1] I understand the experiences of being raised out in the country. By "out in the country," I mean outside of any formally incorporated town or village. My childhood home was at the end of a long gravel driveway, and well out of eyesight of the nearest neighbors. I remember being a part of a comically small high school graduating class. I remember traffic jams caused by a lone, slow-moving piece of farm equipment. In this rural environment, minorities were like shopping malls; the nearest one was 50 minutes away in the "big city." If you, the reader, also come from a rural background, then I feel comfortable stating that we share a mindset that comes from a shared rural upbringing.

I understand your confusion surrounding modern conversations of race and privilege. Why is this still an issue worth talking about? After all, you treat everyone the same, regardless of skin color. You don't discriminate against anyone, and you certainly know that it is wrong to use "the N-word." You haven't done anything to anyone…so how could you still be on the hook for ancient history? Why do some people continually try to "rub it in?" Nowadays the laws are fair, hiring and firing is fair, segregation is illegal… We even elected a black president! You've gotten past race… Why hasn't everyone else?[2]

First, take a deep breath and realize that you're in no position to make declarations on the status of equality. From your rural perch, you have seen exactly one culture: white culture. You haven't had any meaningful interactions with people that don't look and talk like you. Your county, your social circle, and your school district are all nearly 100% white. You have no opportunities for deep dialogues about race with those that have a different background. And no, that one black family doesn't make your school district "diverse." You have not "gotten past" race; you just haven't ever had to deal with it.

I know you believe that race doesn't matter to you. This has been true for most of your life, but only because you are surrounded by other white people.

N. D. Hartlep & B. O. Hensley (Eds.), Critical Storytelling in Uncritical Times, 1–5.

It is easy to be "colorblind" when there is an absence of color. In different settings, race would be a more visible and visceral experience. When in a more diverse environment, you cannot help but be influenced by a legacy of bias.[3]

Consider the quiet assumptions that you make when you venture out into the bigger city. Consider the thought process that went into deciding to lock your car doors when two black males walked past. Consider why you assumed that the spanish conversation of two hispanic waiters was about you. Consider the internal recoil you experience when seeing two men kiss. These feelings don't come from experience, but from inexperience. They don't come from knowledge or rational thought, but from presuppositions and, yes, that dreaded word: p-r-e-j-u-d-i-c-e.

This is an important line to hold onto: You are prejudiced. Not everyone *but* you. You. If that makes you nervous, take some solace in knowing that everyone else is as well.

From time to time, you may have laughed with friends about the way that one black woman spoke. Or that meek, timid Asian kid. You told yourself that it wasn't because of their ethnicity but their behaviors that you ostracized or demeaned them. It was their actions, and hey, anyone can change their actions. However, the social rules by which you judge them are not objective, universal truths. These social rules are a construction; people made them. White people. And they benefit those that display certain characteristics and punish those that don't. Your supposedly objective judgments about people haven't been very objective; a white world order has shaped them. And they constantly work behind the scenes to perpetuate white superiority.

These distorted rules are the essence of "whiteness" (Hayes & Hartlep, 2013). Whiteness doesn't describe one's skin tone. It describes the tone of the society in which we all live.[4] It is a mindset that has shaped our daily interactions (Juárez, 2013). Our culture is not completely fair to everyone. As a result of whites being "on top," value judgments have been weaved into the fabric of our culture. For you, these hidden rules are no doubt difficult to see. They are invisible because they are familiar and favor you. They also seem intuitive because they are highly pervasive. Individuals' behaviors, communication styles, beauty standards, personal stories, mannerisms, foods, and attitudes all have social value. Whiteness is an invisible process that reifies dominant group values, conferring status to those it deems normal.[5] This is an ongoing process that you were born into. This is a process that you and everyone else have been reinforcing your whole lives.

Furthermore, this is something that you've been taught not to acknowledge or consider. Privilege was not a topic raised in your rural school. Even addressing it now creates tension and dissonance in "polite" company. If you're feeling dismissive, then your reaction may be evidence of your socialization into this reality.

If you need any convincing that society is wrapped in whiteness, look at some of the invisible and automatic privileges bestowed upon whites.[6] Whites can watch courageous leaders and beautiful models on television with shared skin tone and facial features. Whites can openly carry firearms in public with neither suspicion nor sanction. Whites, if they so desire, also have the ability to live in an area without any minorities, fully insulating themselves from the troubling thoughts that may come as a result of facing their privilege.

You and I both have this privilege. It means that the "even playing field" is a myth. It is tilted in our favor, and it disadvantages minorities and women: They have to work harder to achieve the same level of success. Equal work does not accrue equal reward. Think again about "colorblindness" (i.e., when people assert they treat everyone the same regardless of race or ethnicity). Colorblind narratives fail to account for counterstories of racism. A colorblind outlook perpetuates the meritocratic myth, and it is an attitude brimming with the hallmarks of whiteness.

"But wait," you might say, "How can society expect me to be accountable for all these things? *I* didn't institute these rules!" This sense of white victimhood is normal. But whiteness isn't a personal debt. You are not expected to atone for the sins of your fathers. Instead, whiteness is a societal scourge.

I have a challenge for you today. Consider the contrasts between the way things are, and the way you would like them to be. Now that you are aware of this uneven playing field, how will you proceed? Will you continue on your way, blithely ignorant of the ongoing prejudice? Or will you actively seek out other instances of whiteness and work to disrupt them?

Of course, this practice has been structured to seem unnatural. When you consider the enormity of this challenge, you may throw your hands in the air in exasperation: "What am I to do?" "What is the right answer?" "What am I supposed to say?"

There isn't a straightforward answer, because there isn't an easy solution. Like a rock in a stream, changing the direction of the undercurrent may seem impossible. The mindset of whiteness has been at work for quite some time, and will continue. Rather than trying to be "right," try to identify the "wrongs" of society, complicity, and privilege. Examine your community and the media through a critical lens. Recognize your own knee-jerk assumptions about those different from you. Notice how whites are portrayed in popular media in relation to others. Look for examples of white privilege and the preferential regard that white culture receives.

Get over your aversion to the topic of race and begin talking about it. Start having difficult conversations about privilege and your role in it. Finally, consider how you can disrupt the placid waters of whiteness in others—sending ripples of resistance.

So, are you racist? Yes.[7] Despite your good intentions and disapproval of overtly racist acts, you are immersed in a white-centric society, and you cannot help but be influenced by it. Up until now, you've been reinforcing racist ways of understanding and behaving. Now, it's time to decide what to carry forward and what to leave behind.

NOTES

[1] In this chapter, I will leave racial or ethnic descriptors, such as "black," "white," or "hispanic," uncapitalized. Many choose to capitalize them. These labels are meaningful and can speak to the subjects' lived experiences, revealing more than the average adjective. However, they do not fully define a person any more than an adjective fully defines a noun. Racial descriptors do not comprise a full biography of a person.

[2] In *Dear White America*, Tim Wise (2012) also seeks to reveal topics such as white privilege from the perspective of a fellow white person. His book may prove useful for those seeking further reading.

[3] Personal and societal bias extends far outside the realm of acts of intolerance. For further reading on systemic vestiges of inequality, see *Racism without Racists* by Eduardo Bonilla-Silva (2013).

[4] Richard Dyer's *The Matter of Whiteness* (2005) expands upon this idea further, which is only briefly discussed in this short letter.

[5] The classroom is not exempt from these preferential rules. For further reading on covert racism in an educational setting, please read *Antiracist Education: From Theory to Practice* by Julie Kailin (2002).

[6] Peggy McIntosh (1990) refers to these privileges as an "invisible knapsack." Her perspective provided my first nuanced look into white privilege when I read it at age 23. She provides an in-depth list of invisible privileges that whites don't consider in their day-to-day lives and use unknowingly.

[7] This is a statement of fact, not a statement of defeat. This doesn't forbid you from being a white ally; rather, it opens the door. For further reading on being a white ally, see Brenda Juárez's (2013) chapter "Learning to Take the Bullet and More" in Cleveland Hayes and Nicholas Hartlep's (2013) *Unhooking from Whiteness: The Key to Dismantling Racism in the United States*.

REFERENCES

Bonilla-Silva, E. (2013). *Racism without racists: Color-blind racism and the persistence of racial inequality in America* (4th ed.). Lanham, MD: Rowman & Littlefield.

Dyer, R. (2005). The matter of whiteness. In P. S. Rothenberg (Ed.), *White privilege: Essential readings on the other side of racism* (pp. 9–14). New York, NY: Worth.

Hayes, C., & Hartlep, N. (Eds.). (2013). *Unhooking from Whiteness: The key to dismantling racism in the United States*. Rotterdam, The Netherlands: Sense Publishers. Retrieved from http://dx.doi.org/10.1007/978-94-6209-377-5

Juárez, B. (2013). Learning to take the bullet and more. In C. Hayes & N. Hartlep (Eds.), *Unhooking from Whiteness: The key to dismantling racism in the United States* (pp. 44–51). Rotterdam, The Netherlands: Sense Publishers. Retrieved from http://dx.doi.org/10.1007/978-94-6209-377-5_3

Kailin, J. (2002). *Antiracist education: From theory to practice*. Lanham, MD: Rowman & Littlefield.

McIntosh, P. (1990). White privilege: Unpacking the invisible knapsack. *Independent School, 49*(2), 31.

Wise, T. J. (2012). *Dear White America: Letter to a new minority*. San Francisco, CA: City Lights Books.

NICHOLAS D. HARTLEP

2. KARMA DOESN'T HAVE TO BE A BITCH

Justice-Oriented Lessons I Learned through Death and Introspection

I regularly ask my teacher education students[1] to share about their K–12 school experiences. I ask them to reflect publicly before their peers in class on the learning experiences they had while in elementary, middle, and high school. It has been my practice to ask my post-secondary students— "Describe your K–12 schooling experience." "Was it overall 'positive' or overall 'negative'?"—ever since I began teaching at the University of Wisconsin at Milwaukee while working on my doctorate in 2008. Over the course of seven years, I have noticed a pattern in my students' responses: the majority recall enjoying K–12 school, which I suspect partially explains why many share their wish to become teachers.

I sincerely believe that my teacher education students, like most pre-service teachers, want their future K–12 students to have equally fond social and positive educational experiences as they did. Yet as I (e.g., see Hartlep, 2013) and others have written elsewhere (Haberman, 2010), despite these teachers' good intentions, typically it is poor and minority students who bear the brunt of racist, culturally insensitive, and ineffective pedagogical practice, not the mainly middle-class white females who are supposedly doing the teaching.[2]

Therefore, I am not concerned whether or not my college students consider themselves to be good, well intentioned, and "personally responsible" citizens (Westheimer & Kahne, 2004). What concerns me most is the frequency with which my students have a difficult time recognizing—or are ignorant of the reality—that their "positive" response often means that they profess loving a system that harms and endangers the lives of the very students they seem so impassioned to inspire and teach (Hayes & Hartlep, 2013).

My teacher education students are shocked and challenged when I share videos with them that support my seemingly "heretical" claim that K–12 teachers who have had a positive schooling experience may be less effective at teaching than K–12 teachers who did not have such positive experiences as students; indeed, the former might be hampered by a narrower understanding of youth and what it means to be young in contemporary contexts. Mostly,

N. D. Hartlep & B. O. Hensley (Eds.), Critical Storytelling in Uncritical Times, 7–20.

my students have a hard time believing that their students—current and future—could possibly be harmed or endangered by the formal schooling process. This stems from where many Illinois State University students come from—towns such as Naperville, IL in Chicago's southern suburbs: privileged spaces.

Foundations of Education courses typically teach critical facts and information that teacher training often overlooks. As a result, processing such jolting information can be challenging for people, especially when (and if) it pushes back against their common sense, or causes "cognitive dissonance." My students experience cognitive dissonance, or extensive mental stress, when they are confronted by new information that conflicts with their existing beliefs, ideas, and values (e.g., that meritocracy is a farce, racism is real and not aberrational, and white privilege does truly exist).

Make no mistake: I use the words "harm" and "endanger" purposefully— not on a whim or for rhetorical or hyperbolic purposes—because it is well documented in the literature (see Olson, 2009; Woodson, 1933). But what do I mean, specifically? The student harm and endangerment to which I refer are the ways in which school—that is, the process of formal K–12 schooling as an institution—socializes "docile bodies" (Foucault, 1995, p. 135) who will not question the established order but will actually reinforce and perpetuate it. To me, the compulsory aspect of public schooling is the essence of the hegemonic socializing system. Meanwhile, the act of branding and selling school to be important, and mandating attendance, ensures that students will be indoctrinated to accept the ideas that the ruling class wishes to legitimize (Alinsky, 1971). This educational process does not lead to critical thinkers or self-determined citizens.

The result of hegemonic schooling practices (such as mandatory attendance policies and surveillance of student bodies in school), matched with equally proselytized and dogmatic teaching, is that "[c]hildren enter school as question marks and leave as periods" (p. 60), according to Neil Postman and Weingartner (1969). As a Cultural Foundations of Education teacher educator, I want my teacher education students to be critical questioners and purveyors of justice-oriented, transformative, and problem-posing teaching practices (Hartlep, 2014; Tutwiler et al., 2013).

The Harm of Hegemony

Meanwhile, despite legislation named otherwise—such as the "No Child Left Behind" Act (NCLB)—there are in fact many children who *are left behind* in schools, and many of these left behind students are non-English speakers, children from poor families, and minorities. Schools further harm K–12 youth when those youth are intentionally "mis-educated"[3] (Woodson, 1933) or "tracked" (Oakes, 1985) by their teachers. Despite research that indicates that de-tracking does not harm high-achieving students but actually helps all students of all abilities, the practice of tracking remains the rule rather than the exception (e.g. see Burris, 2014). Students are also harmed when their classmates bully them, and teachers in a position to help cast a blind eye (Hensley, 2011).

Moreover, most would agree with me that students are also harmed if they get caught in the web of the "prison industrial complex" (Alexander, 2010). Most explicitly, though, I would say that K–12 students are harmed by teachers who, knowingly or unknowingly, reproduce educational and social inequality within their classrooms. Martin Haberman states that K–12 teachers reproduce educational and social inequality by practicing a "pedagogy of poverty." According to Haberman (1991), the pedagogy of poverty refers to 14 practices that are associated with teaching. These practices are as follows: (1) giving information, (2) asking questions, (3) giving directions, (4) making assignments, (5) monitoring seatwork, (6) reviewing assignments, (7) giving tests, (8) reviewing tests, (9) assigning homework, (10) reviewing homework, (11) settling disputes, (12) punishing noncompliance, (13) marking papers, and (14) giving grades. Pedagogies of poverty, critical education, and hegemony are areas with which I, as a Cultural Foundations of Education professor, am most concerned.

Foundations of Education Lenses

When presenting my Social Foundations of Education curriculum to my undergraduate students and my Cultural Foundations of Education curriculum to my doctoral students, I, like other Foundations faculty, teach via critical, interpretive, and normative (see Figure 1) lenses.[4]

Of the three lenses my undergraduate students have the most difficulty receiving and processing material that is overly critical. For instance, many of my teacher education students balk at me when I tell them that the United States' Federal Government paid for pro-NCLB advertising in order to influence public perception of said policy (see Elliott, 2005). Indeed, Orlowski (2011) discusses how hegemony functions through language and spin-doctoring. The "power of language" that Orlowski (2011) refers to in his book *Teaching About Hegemony: Race, Class and Democracy in*

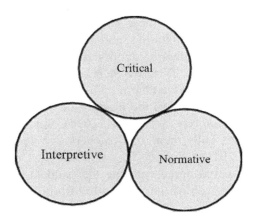

Figure 1. Lenses frequently employed in foundations of education

the 21st Century may be partially responsible for why my undergraduate students have a hard time believing that an educational policy that is supposed to help all children—the so-called No Child Left Behind Act— would require positive advertising by its authors. Similarly, it would be difficult for lay people to believe that the "'Clear Skies Act,' despite its name, enables polluting corporations to increase the amount of toxins they produce," or that the "'Healthy Forests Restoration Act' allows for forests to be clear-cut" (Orlowski, 2011, p. 162).

HOW TO READ THIS CHAPTER

The purpose of my chapter is to demonstrate that in addition to the three standard lenses introduced above—critical, interpretive, and normative— "fiction" may be a useful lens for Social and Cultural Foundations of Education scholars to employ in their teaching and scholarship (see Figure 2).

In this chapter I share my personal experience of being bullied in high school by a boy named Tom (a pseudonym), and of my coming to terms when he died 12 years later. While it is true that Tom really existed and really did die, I fictionalize what might transpire if a reincarnated Tom attended my Cultural Foundations of Education graduate course. To ground my chapter, I draw on Banks and Banks' (1998) suggestion to incorporate fiction into social research. In my fictionalized story, based on real-life events, I share "justice-oriented" (Westheimer & Kahne, 2004) lessons that I feel I learned by analyzing Tom's death through my own introspection.

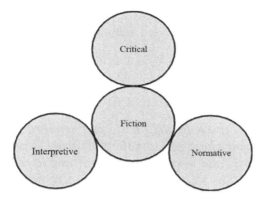

*Figure 2. Fiction as a Nexus for Foundations of Education Lenses
(Adapted from Hartlep & Porfilio, 2015)*

I first share an imaginary journal entry that I might have written as a high school student about my experiences being bullied. I then share a letter, written 12 years later, from the perspective of a 30-year-old me responding to my fictionalized high school journal entry. Next, I imagine what might happen if Tom, the boy who bullied me in high school, were to be reincarnated and become one of my students at Illinois State University. I conclude my chapter by sharing several lessons that I have learned through this introspective process.

I question the traditional expression "Karma's a Bitch," which refers to something that is retributional. In other words, I reject the notion that what "goes around" necessarily has to "come around." My chapter interrupts notions of an "eye for an eye" by arguing that justice-oriented citizenship requires oppressed people to help educate their oppressors about the power of forgiveness and mercy. Like the chapters in Banks and Banks' (1998) edited volume *Fiction & Social Research: By Ice or* Fire—chapters that "experiment with modes of storytelling that consciously attempt to bridge the gaps between author and reader, between fact and truth, between cool reason and hot passion, between the personal and the collective, and between the drama of social life and the legitimized modes of representing it" (p. 7)—my chapter, too, attempts to tell a story to show how I learned to forgive my bully. The story about how I suddenly found myself as his teacher and, in the process, helped educate him about hegemony is obviously a fictional one. Some might dismiss it as a "flight of fancy," out of place in serious academic work, but fiction can be a nexus, connecting the lenses of interpretation, critique, and normalness. Fiction also holds the potential for serving as a "pedagogy of hope" and memory—remembering, retelling, and reconfiguring.

* * *[5]

MAY 12, 2002 [JOURNAL ENTRY]

I cannot wait to leave this hellhole! Fuck! I feel so angry. I am angry because I cannot do anything about my situation at school. I am angry that Tom teases me mercilessly and what he says to me, and does to me, gets under my skin. I have tried to ignore his words and acts, but sometimes I really wish something bad would happen to him. He seems so confident. He should be, I guess, right? No. He should not be! He is a star athlete, and he has a girlfriend who many people say is hot. I don't think she is, considering she has to hide behind makeup, but that is a different story.

I cannot wait to go to college. After this year of high school I am never coming back to Green Bay ever again. I hope Tom doesn't go to UW-Whitewater, where I will be headed next year. I feel so trapped, because I cannot tell people that Tom is bullying me. If I do, he will use that against me, and the teasing will be even worse. I have to stay strong and hide my feelings of hurt, anger, and sadness. I guess this is why I am journaling. Okay, that's enough for now. Until next time.

Nick[6]

MAY 29, 2012 [LETTER TO SELF]

Dear Nick,

I suspect you feel trapped right now, but please trust me when I say that this will all pass. High school is just the beginning of the long road we call life. You have only been alive for 18 years, and you have so much life ahead of you. College is much more accepting of differences of perspective and thought. I bet in ten years you will look back at these high school experiences with a new lease on life. I surely believe that you will have more opportunities, and leaving Green Bay will be healthy for you.

I have never condoned bullying, but did you know that bullies bully people because they don't have a healthy self-concept? Don't believe me? There is actual research that backs this up! Bullies intimidate and bully others to make themselves feel better. Sick logic, isn't it? I know it is difficult to understand, but in many ways these bullies are victims themselves. It does not feel that way, but I bet that if you hang on and persevere, you will go on to do great things. You will be a freedom fighter! Don't let Tom make you doubt yourself. While I don't like Eleanor Roosevelt, she said something wise: "No one can make you feel inferior without your consent."

You're a kind and caring person who is committed to diversity and equity. I know it is natural to do so, but don't allow Tom to pass his insecurities onto you. You are a very secure person and know who you want to become. The world needs you to advocate for freedom, justice, compassion, and love. Stay strong and healthy.

Oh, and here, take a look at these two things I read recently. The first appears on *NPR*—it is titled "Cool Kids Lose, Though it May Take a Few Years." Singh (2014) reports that the student who was cool and popular and was running with the fast crowd is not doing as great later on in life. Tom may appear to have everything together, but you never know what his life will be like after high school. The second read is a journal article. According to Allen, Schad, Oudekerk, and Chango's (2014) article "What Ever Happened to the 'Cool' Kids? Long-Term Sequelae of Early Adolescent Pseudomature Behavior," published in *Child Development*, for "status-seeking teens, reliance upon pseudomature behavior loses its social cachet over time, such that by age 15, early adolescents who engage in high levels of pseudomature behavior no longer have any popularity advantage relative to their peers" (p. 12).

Tom talks about all the sex he is having because he is seeking status—he is most likely inflating each and every time he boasts about sex or anything else that seeks attention.

Nicholas D. Hartlep, Ph.D.[7]

* * *

LESSONS I LEARNED THROUGH DEATH AND INTROSPECTION

While in high school, several individuals in my grade did not show me approval, which caused me to become angry. Mostly I was frustrated because I wanted to be an "insider" rather than an "outsider" to them. In addition to not fitting in socially, I was also bullied. It was a chicken or the egg situation: I am unsure whether I was bullied because I was not approved of, or if the reason I was not approved was because I was bullied. Another thing that bothered me was that while in high school I felt as though I did not do anything to merit the bullying that was perpetrated on me. I felt as though I was innocent and should not have been targeted. Looking back on these high school experiences, I now know many things I did not know back then. One of those being that Asian Americans are teased at higher rates than other minority groups (AALDEF, 2013; American Psychological Association, 2012). Other things I learned through introspection I share below.

Hegemonic forms of masculinity.   A strategy that I employed in an attempt to stave off being bullied as an adolescent was jockeying to gain "insider" status with certain influential groups and people, mainly the jocks. Tom, my bully, was one of the leaders, if not "The Leader," of the jock group. During senior year he was the starting varsity second baseman and quarterback, and he had the approval of many "popular" students—both athletic and academic. However, this hadn't always been the case. For instance, I was the starting pitcher freshman year and one of the main stars on the junior varsity baseball team sophomore year. During this period of time, Tom was a bench warmer. He saw minimal playing time, and even though Tom was below me in terms of rank and success in baseball, I was always friendly toward him. During our sophomore season Tom was indifferent towards me.

The reason Tom did not pitch much during junior varsity was because he had control problems—he could not pitch strikes and would hit batters quite frequently. When Tom and I were on the varsity baseball team as juniors, however, he ended up becoming a starter at second base. Meanwhile, I saw considerably less playing time since I played behind a set of two strong senior pitchers. Neither could I play shortstop like I did during JV, because there was already a two-year starter in that position. When Tom became more successful than me in baseball (e.g., starting at second base, batting well, etc.), he did not extend the same courtesy or treatment to me that I did to him when we were freshmen and sophomores.

It was during this time that Tom began to insult me, tease me, and assert his hyper-masculine identity toward me. He called me "Hot-lips" instead of my real last name "Hartlep." By altering my last name, Tom was intentionally trying to shame me, as if to imply I was not having sex, like he was. Tom's sexual activity with females was something he proudly shared publicly—something that identified him as a jock "getting laid." How did I respond to these moments of teasing and harassment? I internalized hegemonic forms of masculinity (Connell & Messerschmidt, 2005), remained quiet, and began to lift weights religiously, something I never did before.

As I mentioned earlier, Asian Americans endure rates of bullying in high school that outstrip other minorities (American Psychological Association, 2012; National Education Association, 2012). One explanation for why Asian Americans are targeted may be that they are stereotyped as being meek, model-minority nerds who are un-athletic and asexual. But as Donaldson (1993) notes, "The crucial difference between hegemonic masculinity and other forms of other masculinities is not the control of women, but the control of men" (p. 655). Although Tom boasted of his sexual exploits, it wasn't his sex life that I wanted. I wanted his social approval. Because I did not want to be viewed by other high school males (and Tom) as being weak, I began taking store-bought nutritional supplements to increase my muscle mass and definition. I also intentionally did what I could to show to the other males that I was strong and a jock in the weight room—in essence I wanted to be viewed as a man and part of the dominant "insider" group. I recall the first time I bench-pressed 225 lbs in front of others. From their perspective, two "plates" on each side was impressive because I was skinny, but also mostly because the 180 lbs caused the 45-lb bar to bend slightly.

Reflecting on my behavior in high school, I quickly recognize how physically damaging my behavior was, not only to my bodily health—taking muscle-building supplements that are not approved by the FDA—but also for my own psychological wellbeing and self-identity. Also important to note is that during this time I began to feel depressed—I retreated into "gym culture" spending my time to myself lifting weights.[8] Was lifting weights a coping mechanism to deal with my melancholy? What I have described herein has been the reality of a well-known baseball player, Mark McGwire. McGwire is known for having suffered from depression and for taking steroids. While I never took steroids, it is interesting how internalizing hegemonic forms of masculinity is problematic for a variety of reasons for all men. In fact, according to work by Kimmel (1987, 2000), men live under the weight of what it means to "be a man" (the norms of manhood, hegemonic ideals regarding detachment from emotion, and masculine nonverbal behaviors, physicality, and languages of heteronormativity and patriarchy).

Internalized racism and deculturalization. While in high school, I also attempted to distance myself from being perceived as an Asian American. I told anti-Asian jokes with the intent that they would cause my white friends to laugh and like me more. My behavior at this point of my life may well have been "internalized racism" (Lipsky, 1987; Pyke, 2010; Pyke & Dang, 2003). According to Lipsky (1987), internalized racism "is a form of oppression that has been systematically initiated, encouraged, and powerfully enforced by the distress patterns of individual members of the majority culture and their institutions" (p. 3). Lipsky (1987) also notes that internalized racism "has been the primary means by which we have been forced to perpetuate and 'agree' to our own oppression" (p. 1). By telling anti-Asian jokes, I was attempting to distance myself from my own Asian-ness. This act was because I had internalized a feeling of shame for being different than the dominant group—in this case because I was Asian, not white.

Outwardly I did not want anything to do with Korean food or culture, although secretly I did. According to Branch (2012), "Deculturalization is the destruction of the culture of a dominated group and its replacement by the culture of the dominating group" (p. 610). By distancing myself from Korean food, telling jokes that berated what it meant to be Asian in America, and internalizing racism, I was attempting to be cool by deculturalizing my life and replacing it with "hegemonic" masculinity.

Acting cool. Being cool was not something that was related to academics. Intelligence was not worn as a badge. The cool kids were jocks, not those who did well in class.

WELCOMING TOM TO CLASS

If Tom reincarnated and joined my Cultural Foundations of Education course at Illinois State University, how would I treat him? What would my justice-oriented response be to him, especially in the face of my past pain? These are just a few questions I asked myself during discussions in class, while co-editing *Critical Storytelling in Uncritical Times: Stories Disclosed in a Cultural Foundations of Education Course.*

In the movie *Edge of Tomorrow* (2014), actor Tom Cruise is a high-ranking officer in the armed forces. He is labeled a defector, and is sent to serve on the front lines of battle. Cruise is stupefied because the reason he became a high-ranking officer was to avoid seeing enemy fire. In the first battle that Cruise experiences he is killed. However, before he dies on the battlefield, the blood of his killer drips onto him. Cruise quickly learns that the blood dripping on him may be either a blessing or a curse. It may be a blessing because Cruise gets to re-experience life again. It may be a curse, though, because like in the film *Groundhog Day* (1993), his life repeats over and over and over again. Cruise attempts to learn from his mistakes—when he dies, he is reloaded, and he tries to act differently to avoid dying the same way.

I think if Tom, my bully, was brought back to life, it might or might not be like *Edge of Tomorrow.* What do I mean by this? In *Edge of Tomorrow* Cruise has a history that others do not. Cruise knows that he has seen things, while those around him are experiencing it for the first time. Most likely, Tom would not know that he was my bully. The reason is because I concealed it well in high school; I never *publicly* let him feel he got the best of me. However, I would have retained resentment about Tom since he was, in fact, my bully in his previous life. Consequently, if I treated Tom negatively, he would possibly label me an unforgiving asshole, something I do not feel I am. However, if I engaged Tom in becoming a compassionate, empathetic, culturally aware, and non-homophobic human being, I believe I would truly be practicing a justice-oriented pedagogy.

Fiction as a Lens for Cultural Foundations of Education and for Teacher Education

Banks and Banks (1998) indicate that fiction can be a viable and valuable lens to make sense of society and culture. My analysis and the lessons learned through introspection about Tom's death would not have been possible if it weren't for having this lens—fiction—to use. A critical, interpretive, and normative lens would have aided me in analyzing being bullied, but it would not have allowed me to fully grasp what I will discuss in the next section of this chapter: that karma doesn't have to be a bitch.

KARMA DOESN'T HAVE TO BE A BITCH

The overarching justice-oriented lesson that I learned through Tom dying is to not be unfair to others because others are unfair to you. If Tom were to become a graduate student in my Cultural Foundations of Education course, I would do my best to inspire him to be a "question mark" (Postman & Weingartner, 1969). Karma doesn't have to be a bitch, because it wasn't for me. As a high school student I may have dealt with bullying in hegemonic masculine ways, but now—through reflection and my letters to self—I have realized a critical consciousness of compassion.

NOTES

[1] Graduate and/or undergraduate.
[2] Although it is difficult to determine the precise percentage, it is undeniable that many of our nation's K–12 teachers are white and female (e.g., Feistritzer, 2011; Hodgkinson, 2002; Zumwalt & Craig, 2008). For example, according to Feistritzer (2011), 84% of K–12 teachers in the United States are white and 84% are female.
[3] Mis-education refers to how students are taught to believe in things that are untrue.
[4] For more details on the critical, interpretive, and normative lenses, see Standard II (Standards for Academic and Professional Instruction in Foundations of Education, Educational Studies, and Educational Policy Studies, Third Edition, 2013)

[5] Note to reader: These asterisks (* * *) indicate time has passed or a shift in thought has occurred.
[6] Written as an 18-year-old. Back then I went by Nick because I hated the formalized name Nicholas.
[7] Written as a 30-year-old. While in graduate school, I began using the name Nicholas D. Hartlep in all of my writing and legal documents.
[8] I did not seek treatment, so I was not diagnosed officially as having depression.

REFERENCES

Alexander, M. (2010). *The new Jim Crow: Mass incarceration in the age of colorblindness.* New York, NY: The New Press.

Alinsky, S. (1971). *Rules for radicals: A pragmatic primer for realistic radicals.* New York, NY: Vintage.

Allen, J. P., Schad, M. M., Oudekerk, B., & Chango, J. (2014). What ever happened to the "cool" kids? Long-term sequelae of early adolescent pseudomature behavior. *Child Development, 85*(5), 1–15. Retrieved from http://dx.doi.org/10.1111/cdev.12250

American Psychological Association. (2012). Bullying & victimization and Asian American students. Retrieved June 14, 2014, from http://www.apa.org/pi/oema/resources/ethnicity-health/asian-american/bullying-and-victimization.pdf

Asian American Legal Defense Fund (AALDEF). (2013). *One step forward half a step back: A status report on bias-based bullying of Asian American students in New York City schools.* New York, NY: AALDEF. Retrieved June 16, 2014, from http://aaldef.org/2013_NYC_bullying_report.pdf

Banks, A., & Banks, S. P. (Eds.). (1998). *Fiction & social research: By ice or fire.* Walnut Creek, CA: AltaMira.

Branch, A. (2012). Deculturalization. In J. Banks (Ed.), *Encyclopedia of diversity in education* (pp. 610–612). Thousand Oaks, CA: Sage. Retrieved from http://dx.doi.org/10.4135/9781452218533.n190

Burris, C. C. (2014). *On the same track: How schools can join the twenty-first-century struggle against resegregation.* New York, NY: Beacon.

Connell, R. W., & Messerschmidt, J. W. (2005). Hegemonic masculinity: Rethinking the concept. *Gender & Society, 19*(6), 829–859. Retrieved July 12, 2014, from http://www.engagemen-me.org/sites/default/files/Hegemonic%20Masculinity-%20Rethinking%20the%20Concept%20(R.%20W.%20Connell%20and%20James%20W.%20Messerschmidt).pdf

Donaldson, M. (1993). What is hegemonic masculinity? *Theory and Society, 22*(5), 643–657.

Elliott, S. (2005, January 12). A paid endorsement ignites a debate in the public relations industry. *New York Times.* Retrieved June 2, 2014, from http://www.nytimes.com/2005/01/12/business/media/12adco.html?_r=0

Feistritzer, C. E. (2011). *Profiles of teachers in the U.S. 2011.* Washington, DC: National Center for Education Information.

Foucault, M. (1995). *Discipline & punish: The birth of the prison* (2nd ed.). New York, NY: Vintage Books.

Haberman, M. (1991). The pedagogy of poverty versus good teaching. *Phi Delta Kappan, 73*(4), 290–294. Retrieved from https://www.ithaca.edu/compass/pdf/pedagogy.pdf

Haberman, M. (2010). The myth of the "fully qualified" bright young teacher. *American Behavioral Scientist*, *56*(7), 926–940.

Hartlep, N. D. (2013). "The not-so-silent" minority: Scientific racism and the need for epistemological and pedagogical experience in curriculum. In L. William-White, D. Muccular, G. Muccular, & A. F. Brown (Eds.), *Critical consciousness in curricular research: Evidence from the field* (pp. 60–76). New York, NY: Peter Lang.

Hartlep, N. D. (2014). YouTube university: How an educational foundations professor uses critical media in his classroom. In B. Porfilio, J. Gorlewski, P. Thomas, & P. Carr (Eds.), *Social context reform: Equity and opportunity—not accountability—in education reform* (pp. 168–181). New York, NY: Routledge.

Hartlep, N. D., & Porfilio, B. J. (2015). Revitalizing the field of educational foundations and PK–20 educators' commitment to social justice and issues of equity in an age of neoliberalism. *Educational Studies*, *51*(4), 288–304. Retrieved from http://dx.doi.org/10.1080/00131946.2015.1053367

Hayes, C., & Hartlep, N. D. (Eds.). (2013). *Unhooking from whiteness: The key to dismantling racism in the United States*. Rotterdam, The Netherlands: Sense Publishers. Retrieved from http://dx.doi.org/10.1007/978-94-6209-377-5

Hensley, B. O. (2011). Performing heteronormativity, hegemonic masculinity, and constructing a body from bullying. *Florida Communication Journal*, *39*(1), 55–65.

Hodgkinson, H. (2002). Demographics and teacher education: An overview. *Journal of Teacher Education*, *53*(2), 102–105. Retrieved from http://dx.doi.org/10.1177/0022487102053002002

Kimmel, M. (Ed.). (1987). *Changing men: New directions in research on men and masculinity*. Newbury Park, CA: Sage.

Kimmel, M. (2000). *The gendered society*. New York, NY: Oxford University Press.

Lipsky, S. (1987). *Internalized racism*. Seattle, WA: Rational Island Publishers.

National Education Association. (2012, May). API students at increased risk for bullying [Focus on Asian Americans and Pacific Islanders Report]. Retrieved June 8, 2014, from http://www.nea.org/assets/docs/API-StudentsatIncreasedRiskforBullying.pdf

Oakes, J. (1985). *Keeping track: How schools structure inequality*. New Haven, CT: Yale University Press.

Olson, K. (2009). *Wounded by school: Recapturing the joy in learning and standing up to old school culture*. New York, NY: Teachers College Press.

Orlowski, P. (2011). *Teaching about hegemony: Race, class and democracy in the 21st century*. New York, NY: Springer.

Postman, N., & Weingartner, C. (1969). *Teaching as a subversive activity*. New York, NY: Delacorte.

Pyke, K. D. (2010). What is internalized racial oppression and why don't we study it? Acknowledging racism's hidden injuries. *Sociological Perspectives*, *53*(4), 551–572. Retrieved July 14, 2014, from http://irows.ucr.edu/cd/courses/232/pyke/intracopp.pdf

Pyke, K. D., & Dang, T. (2003). "FOB" and "Whitewashed": Identity and internalized racism among second generation Asian Americans. *Qualitative Sociology*, *26*(2), 147–172. Retrieved from http://dx.doi.org/10.1023/A:1022957011866

Singh, M. (2014, June 12). Cool kids lose, though it may take a few years. *NPR*. Retrieved June 20, 2014, from http://www.npr.org/blogs/health/2014/06/12/321314037/cool-kids-lose-though-it-may-take-a-few-years?utm_source=facebook.com&utm_medium=social&utm_campaign=npr&utm_term=nprnews&utm_content=20140612

Tutwiler, S. W., deMarrais, K., Gabbard, D., Hyde, A., Konkol, P., Li, H.,... Swain, A. (2013). Standards for academic and professional instruction in foundations of education, educational studies, and educational policy studies third edition, 2012, draft presented to the educational community by the American educational studies association's committee on academic standards and accreditation. *Educational Studies*, *49*(2), 107–118. Retrieved from http://dx.doi.org/10.1080/00131946.2013.767253

Westheimer, J., & Kahne, J. (2004). Educating the "good" citizen: Political choices and pedagogical goals. *Political Science and Politics*, *37*(2), 241–247.

Woodson, C. G. (1933). *The mis-education of the Negro*. Washington, DC: Associated Publishers.

Zumwalt, K., & Craig, E. (2008). Who is teaching? Does it matter? In M. C. Smith, F. Nemieser, J. D. McIntyre, & K. E. Demers (Eds.), *Handbook of research on teacher education: Enduring questions in changing context* (pp. 404–423). New York, NY: Routledge.

AMANDA ROHAN

3. "MICRO(ACT)GRESSIONS"

Real Lessons Learned from Fake Dialogue

As I walked into the common area of the lab, I looked at the Black woman waiting for the next part of the study and asked, "Are you an athlete here?"

With a smile, the woman replied that she was not an athlete at the university.

I then commented, "I love how you girls can do so many crazy things with your hair; I can only wear mine straight."

She laughed nervously and said, "Thank you."

As we walked to a private room, I asked, "So, have you heard the new Drake album?"[1] Again, her polite answer was accompanied by a short response. I then began the *Stroop Test*, a neuropsychological assessment used to measure executive functioning[2] and cognition.

The utterances shared above are racial microaggressions—insults that occur automatically and that are often unintentional. They happen on a daily basis and maintain a worldview of White supremacy (Sue, Capodilupo, & Holder, 2008). As a White female doctoral student in a psychology graduate program, my role in this research study, conducted on campus, was to deliver racial microaggressions to Black female college students at a Predominantly White Institution (PWI) in an effort to examine their cognitive consequences. While existing research supports the negative physiological and psychological consequences of racial microaggressions, little is known about their immediate cognitive consequences (Smith, Allen, & Danely, 2007). The cognitive consequences of racial microaggressions present an important and understudied area because these consequences potentially can impact academic performance, as well as mental health in general. Because of their covert and unintentional nature, microaggressions present a significant problem for racially diverse students in American schools.

The study described above is a fellow School Psychology doctoral student's ongoing dissertation. Prior to this research, I had only been involved in research projects that focused strictly on academics at the Florida Center for Reading Research, where I administered standardized reading assessments

N. D. Hartlep & B. O. Hensley (Eds.), Critical Storytelling in Uncritical Times, 21–26.

to elementary school students and collected data on reading comprehension. I volunteered to be a confederate[3] in this current research study because the premise and structure of the study were fresh and exciting, and because its use of deception greatly interested me. What I did not know—but quickly learned—was how much this experience would transform me personally and professionally, influencing my development as a budding school psychologist.

FROM ISOLATED TO ACTIVELY EXPOSED

I grew up in the South in a middle-class family. My father is a retired police officer, and my mother stayed at home with my sister and me. I lived in a town and attended primary and secondary schools that were predominantly white. Therefore, before attending college, I had very few experiences with diverse student populations (or diverse populations in general). Moving from my quiet hometown—nestled between the Atlantic coast of Florida and the rural outskirts of Lake Okeechobee—to the more urban state capital, Tallahassee, to attend Florida State University was somewhat of a culture shock. For the first time, I was exposed to a diverse student population by living in the college dormitories, which were filled with students of various racial, economic, and cultural backgrounds. Because of this new environment, I immediately began to establish friendships with more diverse fellow students. Through these friendships, I realized that college presented an amazing opportunity for me to grow as a person and to expose myself to situations and people that were different from me growing up.

Thus, during my undergraduate education I sought out experiences that posed a challenge to my comfort level in terms of race and culture. One of the most educative experiences I had at Florida State was a field experience for an adolescent development course. It was at an alternative education program established in conjunction with the Department of Juvenile Justice. As a mentor to a racially and culturally diverse population of adolescents, it was during this field experience that my dormant passion for social justice was awakened and my desire to be a school psychologist grew.

From my coursework in college, I had general knowledge of the educational disparities of students of color, but working at an alternative education setting—in which over 90 percent of the adolescents were Black—was the first time I had a concrete experience where I was confronted with this disproportionality. The educational disparity that students of color face has also been supported by empirical research. For example, McKinney,

Bartholomew, and Gray (2010) report that students of color, especially Black males, are represented in exclusionary discipline practices (such as school suspension and expulsion) in unbalanced numbers, even though they do not engage in more severe problematic behaviors than White students (as cited by the National Association of School Psychologists, 2012). This is extremely problematic because these disciplinary practices are associated with student dropout rates and entry into the prison system, as demonstrated by my field placement experience.

FAKE DIALOGUE, REAL LESSONS

Fast forward to my current graduate studies at a PWI in the Midwest. As previously mentioned, when I volunteered to be a confederate for the dissertation examining cognitive consequences of racial microaggressions, I did not realize the impact this experience would have on me personally and professionally.

I had my first realization of the power relations in this experience during our rehearsal. Once the university's Institutional Review Board approved the dissertation and its script, we practiced our roles with the doctoral candidate who proposed the study. Despite knowing that we were rehearsing, I experienced physiological reactions: I shook, had intense butterflies in my stomach, and stumbled on my words. After rehearsing, I had these same physiological reactions while running the first participant randomly assigned to the "experimental condition" (i.e., experiencing racial microaggressions). However, this time I had the additional challenge of fighting back tears; knowingly being insensitive to an unsuspecting participant was more difficult than I was mentally prepared for. Fortunately, I was present in the room during every single debriefing portion of the study, and I always apologized profusely to the now "not-so-nervously-laughing" participants: many of the participants remarked that these were comments they heard on a daily basis and had thus learned to laugh it off in order to cope.

For me, this experience not only educated me on what microaggressions are, but also how often they occur and their impact on marginalized individuals. I have become hyperaware of them, seeing them now on a daily basis—a skill I doubt I would have learned had I not served as a confederate in this study. Ultimately, I have learned how microaggressive language can be debilitating, and this experience has been eye-opening for me as a future school psychologist. The subsequent knowledge and awareness I have gained through this experience has made me more culturally competent by helping me to become aware of microaggressions and their impact, especially on racially and culturally diverse students in American school systems.

IMPLICATIONS FOR SCHOOL PSYCHOLOGISTS: WHY IS THIS IMPORTANT?

According to the 2011 U.S. Census Bureau report, there was a 15.4 percent increase in the U.S. population self-identified as Black (i.e., African-American, Caribbean Americans, Black Latino/a, and other ethnic groups who self-identify as Black) from 2000 to 2010. Moreover, information gathered from the U.S. Census Bureau indicated that 50.4 percent of the American population under the age of one was a minority. Given the increasing diversity in the U.S. student population, school psychologists are working within a profession where there is a critical need for culturally responsive psychological services (Merrell, Ervin, & Peacock, 2012). This need is also amplified by the fact that the majority (55.6%) of the members of the National Association of School Psychologists (NASP) self-identify as White (INFOCUS Marketing, 2014). Additionally, when considering the national demographics of school psychologists and including those who are not members of NASP, Merrell and colleagues report that 92.6 percent of school psychologists are European American (Merrell, Ervin, & Peacock, 2012).

The NASP "Position Statement on Racism, Prejudice, and Discrimination" emphasizes the role of school psychologists as agents of change in children's lives and their responsibility to advocate for equity through the encouragement of social justice efforts that support the academic, social, and emotional needs of all students within the American school system (National Association of School Psychologists, 2012). According to Ong, Phinney, and Dennis (2006), students who have experienced racism, prejudice, and discrimination exhibit more resilience when they encounter high expectations; have support from their parents, their school, and their community; and have a strong sense of racial or ethnic identity (as cited by NASP, 2012, p. 2). Thus, school psychologists should work to promote positive school environments for students, integrating a "social justice lens into all educational environments" (NASP, 2012, p. 2). This is especially important because according to Davis, Aronson, and Salinas (2006), stereotypes, which result in the use of microaggressions, have the potential to culminate in self-fulfilling prophecies and, consequently, lower academic achievement and other negative outcomes (as cited by NASP, 2012).

Engaging in perspective-taking on behalf of diverse students with whom school psychologists work is one way to employ culturally-responsive practices. Since culture relates to factors other than race—such as religion, sexual orientation, socioeconomic status, neighborhood, family composition, etc.—school psychologists benefit from being aware of their worldviews and monitoring the influence they have on their professional practice. This can be accomplished by reflecting on one's lived experiences and personal background.

By reflecting on my lived experiences, I have embraced perspective-taking during my graduate training. Serving as a confederate in the anteroom has made me more aware of my worldviews and has provided me with knowledge of racial microaggressions. School psychologists need to be conscious of the fact that even well-meaning people can be unintentionally offensive through microaggressive behavior while working with diverse populations of students. Awareness will begin to help school psychologists promote positive and supportive school environments, thereby enhancing the psychological, social, and academic functioning and overall wellbeing of all students.

NOTES

[1] Drake is a popular contemporary rap music artist who is a Black male.
[2] Executive functioning refers to overall cognitive processing that includes working memory, reasoning, planning, and problem solving.
[3] A research confederate is an actor who participates in a research study along with the participant, although data is not collected from the confederate. The use of a confederate involves deception, which must be addressed during debriefing that takes place at the conclusion of the study.

REFERENCES

Davis, C., Aronson, J., & Salinas, M. (2006). Shades of threat: Racial identity as a moderator of stereotype threat. *Journal of Black Psychology, 32*, 399–417. Retrieved from http://dx.doi.org/10.1177/0095798406292464

INFOCUS Marketing. (2014). Retrieved June 8, 2014, from http://www.infocusmarketing.com/lists/nasp?type=1

McKinney, E., Bartholemew, C., & Gray, L. (2010). RTI and SWPBIS: Confronting the problem of disproportionality. *Communiqué, 38*(6), 26–29. Retrieved June 16, 2014, from http://www.sociallearningcenter.org/uploads/CQMarApr2010.pdf

Merrell, K. W., Ervin, R. A., & Peacock, G. G. (2012). *School psychology for the 21st century: Foundations and practices* (2nd ed.). New York, NY: Guilford Press.

National Association of School Psychologists. (2012). *NASP position statement on racism, prejudice, and discrimination*. Retrieved June 16, 2014, from http://www.nasponline.org/about_nasp/positionpapers/RacismPrejudice.pdf

Ong, A. D., Phinney, J. S., & Dennis, J. (2006). Competence under challenge: Exploring the protective influence of parental support and ethnic identity in Latino college students. *Journal of Adolescence, 29*, 961–979. Retrieved from http://dx.doi.org/10.1016/j.adolescence.2006.04.010

Smith, W. A., Allen, W. R., & Danley, L. L. (2007). "Assume the position…you fit the description" psychosocial experiences and racial battle fatigue among African American male college students. *American Behavioral Scientist, 51*(4), 551–578. Retrieved from http://dx.doi.org/10.1177/0002764207307742

Sue, D. W., Capodilupo, C. M., & Holder, A. (2008). Racial microaggressions in the life experience of Black Americans. *Professional Psychology: Research and Practice, 39*(3), 329. Retrieved from http://dx.doi.org/10.1037/0735-7028.39.3.329

United States Census Bureau. (2011a). *The black population: 2010*. Retrieved June 2, 2014, from http://www.census.gov/prod/cen2010/briefs/c2010br-06.pdf

United States Census Bureau. (2011b). *The white population: 2010*. Retrieved June 11, 2014, from http://www.census.gov/prod/cen2010/briefs/c2010br-05.pdf

United States Census Bureau. (2012). *Most children younger than age 1 are minorities, Census Bureau reports*. Retrieved June 2, 2014, from http://www.census.gov/newsroom/releases/archives/population/eb12-90.html

KATHLEEN O'BRIEN

4. "MIS-EDUCATION"

Why Teachers Need Foundations of Education Courses

> The problem does not always start in kindergarten, as is often assumed, but in the university, 'the true founding-stone of all education,' where those who will carry out the functions for our society are trained to set the standards for all.
>
> W.E.B. Du Bois (paraphrased in Kailin, 2002, p. 23)

SETTING THE STAGE

During my second year teaching in District 2, and my first year teaching first grade at Chant Elementary, I found myself sitting in the audience in support of a colleague's annual end-of-the-year play. I hesitated attending because I was critical of the scripted curriculum Mrs. Krendall[1] followed with her first-grade students. For this reason, I resisted her previous invitations to co-teach, although I highly value collaboration if it benefits students.

Another source of my resistance was to the production itself—*Snow White*. Adaptions of this play exist that are critical and multicultural. Further, Delpit (1995) discusses the value of students writing their own plays. My students were extremely excited about *Snow White* because their friends in the other first-grade classroom were in the performance and repeatedly requested our participation. I assumed Mrs. Krendall's students were learning valuable literacy skills and enhancing their self-efficacy through the production, and the experience of viewing the performance would support my students' social skills. I also believed that attending would extend our learning community. For all these reasons, and as a teacher who practices sociocultural methodologies, I believed attending the play was worthwhile.

Snow White

On the day of the play, I sat down in the gym with my students for the practice rehearsal. I watched as various key characters came to the microphone, shared

N. D. Hartlep & B. O. Hensley (Eds.), Critical Storytelling in Uncritical Times, 27–35.

lines, and then descended into the background. I watched my students' body language. They were engaged while listening to and watching a familiar story enacted by their recess friends.

I watched as five Black[2] boys stood tall as trees in the background. My initial enjoyment shifted as internal alarms sounded. My critical lens caused me to question how these child actors were being socialized, how the audience was being socialized, and how their families would feel upon watching this performance. Unfortunately, what followed only reinforced stereotypes of Black boys (Giroux, 2003; Kitwana, 2002; Ladson-Billings, 1995; Noguera, 2009; Perry, 2003; Webb-Johnson, 2002).

The children who had key roles were all blonde-haired and blue-eyed. My mind and heart raced; how could this possibly happen? I concluded that this *just happens* when teachers fail to examine their own teaching practices in a white supremacist society. A veteran teacher at Chant Elementary with thirty years of experience, and currently on the brink of retirement, produced this racist theatrical performance.

I wondered: How many students in Mrs. Krendall's career—through her own dysconscious racism (King & Ladson-Billings, 1990) or "white pathology" (Jackson, 2011)—were mis-educated (Woodson, 2000) vis-à-vis images of Black boys standing in as trees while the blonde-haired, blue-eyed children were the stars of the show? When we got back to the classroom I asked my students what they noticed. One student replied, "I noticed that all the trees were all Black boys." This student had the perceptiveness to notice something that her classmates overlooked. The tone of her voice was tinged with sadness.

I shared my student's and my observations with Ms. Guzman (my principal) and how I thought families might react, as they would be watching the play later that evening. She responded with exasperation, "Ya think?" When I asked if she did anything to address this, Ms. Guzman responded that it was part of her responsibility as principal of the school to address teachers' methods of instruction in evaluations and to meet with teachers.

I was relieved that Ms. Guzman was aware of the racism in Mrs. Krendall's rendition of *Snow White* because in my previous experiences, principals have been unaware of hegemonic discourses and the power relations in their schools. Administrators are often purveyors of hegemony in school (Chapman, Joseph, Hartlep, Vang, & Lipsey, 2014). Needless to say, my critical "observations" hadn't always been well received by uncritical school administrators. Because I wanted to keep my teaching job, I didn't alienate my principal by pointing out something she didn't see (or want to see), much less address.

While her response was better than I had originally anticipated, I still wanted more to be done. *The play should have been canceled. She should have observed the play before this point and intervened.* Ms. Guzman felt she had to create and maintain working relationships with her building teachers, so I understood why she needed to "keep the peace" rather than make a likely unpopular decision. *Still, would canceling the play really fix the problem?*

I always found the atmosphere of elementary schools to be politically palpable. I recall the familiar "walking-on-eggshells" dance around teacher philosophies, practices, and the "way we do things around here." For this reason, I am always surprised (and at the same time not surprised) when I hear, "Schools aren't political. They're neutral." I'm surprised because it seems obvious and strange that parents, students, and teachers rarely talk about the reality that schools are political, nor do they take any practical steps to ensure the democratic pillars—which supposedly distinguish education in our country—are enacted.

As Kailin (2002) asserts, "Teachers are not simply mechanical devices through which knowledge is imparted: rather they are also change agents who creatively interact with their students, learning from them as well as instructing them" (p. 56). The system we live in and learn within perpetuates apathy, ignorance, systematic oppression, and has devastating consequences for disenfranchised and marginalized groups who, in turn, are then blamed for the system and its outcomes (Fine, 1991). Policies, practices, and decisions— i.e., curriculum development, school funding (Darling-Hammond, 2006), programs used to track, reward, and punish "desirable" behaviors, power distribution within classrooms, and the system at large—are all emblematic of schools-as-political-systems. The most dangerous thing is not *what* students are taught, but *how* they are taught. Farber (1969) refers to "clever robots" (p. 37) produced after twelve years of indoctrination or schooling, drawing attention to the ways students are socialized to please authority figures and to learn isolated facts devoid of critical thinking. Students trained in this manner are perfect for maintaining systems of oppression in a society.

EPISTEMOLOGY IS POLITICAL

Being white and a female made me part of the dominant teacher demographic. I realized I needed to use critical pedagogy/literacy (Tejeda, 2000) as a lens through which to teach as a result of the coursework in my Master's in Reading program. Although I didn't consider my first-grade classroom to be racially or ethnically diverse—fifteen students were white, five were

African American, and two were multiracial—I still actively taught critical multicultural education because it benefited all my students. As Nieto and Bode (2012) postulate, "It can even be convincingly argued that students from the dominant culture need multicultural education more than others because they are generally the most miseducated or undereducated about diversity" (p. 49).

The same mis-education or under-education is true for teacher preparation. With 84% of the teaching force in America comprised of white females (Zumwalt & Craig, 2008), it is racist not to expose pre-service teachers to anti-racist curriculum. Institutionalized racism is perpetuated in schools of education when, for instance, programs have diversity standards, but only one course is required that addresses racism and normativity[3] in all its forms.

Most of my Social Foundations of Education students have completed almost all of their pre-service coursework, and student teaching is the last remaining component of their preparation before becoming teachers. Social Foundations of Education is likely the only curricular moment in a teacher's preparation that they will examine privilege and stereotypes, consider counterstories to deficit theorizing, and view students through asset-based lenses (Yosso, 2005).

Jackson (2011) describes the ways uninterrogated notions of whiteness can manifest: "Whites…who benefit in real and tangible ways from that system, are also disenfranchised as both participants in and beneficiaries of a racially oppressive power structure" (p. 436). Jackson goes on to say that "if whites are not made privy to the unfinished business of racial progress as early as possible, they stand to experience trauma, cognitive dissonance, emotional devastation, identity crisis, and the embodiment of white pathology" (p. 450). With most of our nation's teachers being white, interrupting this cycle seems of the utmost importance.

The political nature of epistemology is demonstrated at the classroom level when teachers choose to (or not to) co-construct knowledge and center what counts as knowledge around what students already know and bring to the classroom. Epistemology refers to ways of knowing, which include *what knowledge* is valued and *how knowledge* comes to be known and applied.

Drawing on students' knowledge as a springboard from which to inform further learning communicates value and worth about what they know, leading to efficacy. There is a myth that the only valuable knowledge is what aligns with standards of learning and accountability. Contrary to this myth, students' knowledge *can* be assessed and used as learning platforms. For example, after reading in the content areas (science, math, social studies), students can collectively create charts that could help them read, write, and solve math problems (Delpit, 1995), as opposed to displaying commercially produced charts with predetermined content. Local and national standards-based content and learning requirements can be added to these student-crafted charts. Student generated charts showcase and bridge students' knowledge—inclusive of home and community values—to academic knowledge (Delpit, 1995, 2002, 2006; Gutiérrez & Rogoff, 2003; Ladson-Billings, 1995). In this way, students, drawing upon their "funds of knowledge" (Moll, 1992) and their "cultural capital" (Yosso, 2005), are knowledge producers rather than knowledge consumers. Epistemology is political because knowledge must be questioned, critiqued, and co-constructed.

DISTRICT 2, CHANT ELEMENTARY, AND OUR CLASS

District 2 is located in a town with two colleges, both of which have teacher preparation programs. Pre-service teachers are frequently "learning" to be teachers by volunteering, completing clinical hours, and student teaching within this school district. District 2 is racially, ethnically, and socioeconomically diverse (Illinois Report Card, 2014). The corporate presence within the community draws employees from other countries and whose children know little English. Many of the community's African American and Mexican American members are segregated both racially and economically on the west side of town. There are clear economic and racial lines drawn geographically between high-poverty areas and the spaces where the employees of the universities and corporations live. As seen in many towns throughout Illinois (cf. Loewen, 2005), segregation was the result of housing and employment discrimination (Coates, 2014; Pratt, 2014).

Chant Elementary, where I taught, had a Mexican American population of 34.5% (Illinois State Report Card, 2014), and is designated the "bilingual" school in the district. Each grade level has one or two bilingual classrooms—depending on the number of students—that share some classes (P.E. and Music) with the non-bilingual classes. The non-bilingual classes were made up of 39.1% white, 15.2% African American, and 9.1% multiracial students. Low-income students comprised 76.4% of the student body (Illinois State Report Card, 2014). I taught first-grade in a non-bilingual class, and as mentioned earlier, it was not racially or ethnically diverse from my perspective. The faculty and staff at Chant were predominantly white, except for two Mexican American teachers and our principal (who was from Argentina). The other bilingual teachers were white, but had earned their bilingual certificates in college.

SOCIAL AND CULTURAL FOUNDATIONS OF EDUCATION COURSES

I share my story to underscore the need for pre-service teachers to take courses like Social Foundations of Education and to learn about culturally-relevant pedagogy as well as how power plays out in school (Delpit, 1998; Gay, 2000; King & Ladson-Billings, 1990; Ladson-Billings, 1992; Marx, 2006). I do not imply that Foundations courses even begin to address the massive societal change needed to provide level playing fields for people of color in America (Delpit, 1998): "Bell (1995) contends that progress toward racial equality for blacks (and all people of color) is contingent upon the degree to which whites are calculated to benefit from that progress" (as cited in Jackson, 2011, p. 437). In other words, changes towards racial equality won't happen unless interests converge (*cf.* Bell, 1995).

I believe Foundations coursework makes teachers more aware of stereotypes, racism, discrimination, dominant group oppression, and their impact on students, especially white teachers who have primarily lived in and interacted within homogenous communities (Ullucci, 2011). Because anti-racist and anti-oppressive education is absent in most K–12 classrooms, and whiteness invisible to most white people, these courses are imperative in teacher preparation programs. According to Gay (2000), culturally relevant pedagogy is needed because it challenges the *status quo* and it "develops in students an intolerance for all kinds of oppression, discrimination, and exploitation, as well as the moral courage to act in promoting academic, social, cultural, and political justice among ethnic groups" (p. 214).

I understand that countering assumptions about normativity is an ongoing and life-long process. Ideally pre-service and practicing teachers would have multiple Foundations of Education courses throughout their educations and careers. The foci of these Foundations courses may include (but are not limited to) the following: (a) antiracist education, (b) critical analysis of equity and power in schooling, (c) continual self- and pedagogically-reflective practices, (d) familiarity with data that contradicts hegemonic discourses, (e) stereotypes, (f) all forms of deficit thinking, (g) listening to counternarratives and history that's been left out, (h) critical whiteness studies, and (i) asset-based paradigms (Boler, 1999; Gorski, Zenkov, Osei-Kofi, & Sapp, 2013; Kailin, 2002; Marx, 2006; Trifonas, 2003; Valencia, 2010; Yosso, 2005).

Mrs. Krendall retired three years later. Ms. Guzman moved to a dual-language school on the West coast the summer after the *Snow White* production. She was replaced by a veteran principal of the district who didn't share the same philosophy as Ms. Guzman, meaning that the veteran principal probably didn't follow up on the meeting that took place between Ms. Guzman and Mrs. Krendall about producing racist plays. The epigraph in this chapter omits the fact that all schooling, no matter the level, is representative of the society in which it functions. Du Bois draws attention to the power the university holds in educating pre-service teachers, and the power teachers have as socializing agents in schools. Teachers need Foundations of Education courses to grow their perspectives and examine hegemony. Myers (1987) says, "[P]ower is the ability to define reality" (p. 79). Black boys should define their own realities, and not have a racist teacher do it for them; they should have starring roles too.

NOTES

[1] All names are pseudonyms.
[2] According to Kailin (2002), "Conventions in publishing dictate that if Black is capitalized, then white must also be capitalized. I disagree with this convention because I think it is a false comparison. The capitalization of terms identifying people of color is important for legitimation and recognition, especially for those who have suffered racial or ethnic discrimination in a white supremacist context" (p. xix). I agree with her, so I choose to capitalize Black, but not white in this chapter.
[3] I am referring to heteronormativity: nondisabled, thin, white, male, class and economic privilege, English speaking, American, U.S.-born, Christian, and Eurocentric epistemologies.

REFERENCES

Bell, D. A. (1995). Brown v Board of education and the interest convergence dilemma. In K. Crenshaw, N. Gotanda, G. Peller, & K. Thomas (Eds.), *Critical race theory: The key writings that formed the movement* (pp. 20–29). New York, NY: The New Press.

Boler, M. (1999). *Feeling power: Emotions and education.* New York, NY: Routledge.

Chapman, T. K., Joseph, T., Hartlep, N., Vang, M., & Lipsey, T. (2014). The double-edged sword of curriculum: How curriculum in majority white suburban high schools supports and hinders the growth of students of color. *Curriculum and Teaching Dialogue, 16*(1&2), 87–101.

Coates, T. (2014, May). The case for reparations. *The Atlantic.* Retrieved from http://www.theatlantic.com/features/archive/2014/05/the-case-for-reparations/361631/

Darling-Hammond, L. (2006). Securing the right to learn: Policy and practice for powerful teaching and learning. *Educational Researcher, 35*(7), 13–24. Retrieved from http://dx.doi.org/10.3102/0013189X035007013

Delpit, L. (1995). *Other people's children: Cultural conflict in the classroom.* New York, NY: The New Press.

Delpit, L. (1998). The silenced dialogue: Power and pedagogy in educating other peoples' children. *Harvard Educational Review, 58*(3), 280–298.

Delpit, L. (2002). In L. Delpit & J. K. Dowdy (Eds.), *The skin that we speak: Thoughts on language and culture in the classroom* (pp. 31–48). New York, NY: The New Press.

Delpit, L. (2006). Lessons from teachers. *Journal of Teacher Education, 57*(3), 220–231. http://dx.doi.org/10.1177/0022487105285966

Farber, J. (1969). *The student as nigger: Essay and stories*. North Hollywood, CA: Contact Books.

Fine, M. (1991). *Framing dropouts: Notes on the politics of an urban public high school*. Albany, NY: State University of New York.

Gay, G. (2000). *Culturally responsive teaching: Theory, research, and practice*. New York, NY: Teachers College Press.

Giroux, H. (2003). Pedagogies of difference, race, and representation: Film as a site of translation politics. In P. P. Trifonas (Ed.), *Pedagogies of difference: Rethinking education for social change* (pp. 83–109). New York, NY: RoutledgeFalmer.

Gorski, P. C., Zenkov, K., Osei-Kofi, N., & Sapp, J. (Eds.). (2013). *Cultivating social justice teachers: How teacher educators have helped students overcome cognitive bottlenecks and learn critical social justice concepts*. Sterling, VA: Stylus.

Gutiérrez, K. D., & Rogoff, B. (2003). Cultural ways of learning: Individual traits or repertoires of practice. *Educational Researcher, 32*(5), 19–25. Retrieved from http://dx.doi.org/10.3102/0013189X032005019

Illinois Report Card. (2014). Retrieved from www.illinoisreportcard.com

Jackson, T. A. (2011). Which interests are served by the principle of interest convergence? Whiteness, collective trauma, and the case for anti-racism. *Race, Ethnicity, and Education, 14*(4), 435–459. Retrieved from http://dx.doi.org/10.1080/13613324.2010.548375

Kailin, J. (2002). *Antiracist education: From theory to practice*. Lanham, MD: Rowman & Littlefield.

King, J. E., & Ladson-Billings, G. (1990). The teacher education challenge in elite university settings: Developing critical perspectives for teaching in a democratic and multicultural society. *European Journal of Intercultural Studies, 1*(2), 15–30. Retrieved from http://dx.doi.org/10.1080/0952391900010202

Kitwana, B. (2002). Race war: Policing, incarceration, and the containment of Black youth. In W. Ayers, G. Ladson-Billings, G. Michie, & P. Noguera (Eds.), *City kids, city schools: More reports from the front row* (pp. 294–304). New York, NY: The New Press.

Ladson-Billings, G. (1992). Liberatory consequences of literacy: A case of culturally relevant instruction for African American students. *The Journal of Negro Education, 61*(3), 374–379. Retrieved from http://dx.doi.org/10.2307/2295255

Ladson-Billings, G. (1995). Toward a theory of culturally relevant pedagogy. *American Educational Research Journal, 32*(3), 465–491. Retrieved from http://dx.org/10.3102/00028312032003465

Loewen, J. W. (2005). *Sundown towns: A hidden dimension of American racism*. New York, NY: Touchstone.

Marx, S. (2006). *Revealing the invisible: Confronting passive racism in teacher education*. New York, NY: Routledge.

Moll, L. C. (1992). Literacy research in community and classrooms: A sociocultural approach. In R. Beach, J. L. Green, M. L. Kamil, & T. Shanahan (Eds.), *Multidisciplinary perspectives on literacy research* (pp. 179–207). Urbana, IL: National Council of Teachers of English.

Myers, L. J. (1987). The deep structure of culture: Relevance of traditional African culture in contemporary life. *Journal of Black Studies, 18*(1), 72–85. Retrieved from http://dx.doi.org/10.1177/002193478701800105

Nieto, S., & Bode, P. (2012). *Affirming diversity: The sociopolitical context of multicultural education*. Boston, MA: Pearson.

Noguera, P. (2009). *The trouble with Black boys: And other reflections on race, equity, and the future of public education*. San Francisco, CA: Jossey-Bass.

Perry, T. (2003). Up from the parched earth. Toward a theory of African-American achievement. In T. Perry, C. Steele, & A. G. Hilliard III (Eds.), *Young, gifted, and Black: Promoting high achievement among African-American students* (pp. 1–108). Boston, MA: Beacon.

Pratt, M. (2014). Turning points in African American history in Bloomington-Normal, IL. *Illinois History Teacher, 7*(1). Retrieved June 23, 2014, from http://www.lib.niu.edu/1999/ihtlist99.html

Tejeda, C. (2000). Toward a spatialized understanding of the Chicana(o)/Latina(o) educational experience: Theorizations of space and the mapping of educational outcomes in Los Angeles. In C. Tejeda, C. Martinez, & Z. Leonardo (Eds.), *Charting new terrains of Chicana(o)/Latina(o) education* (pp. 131–161). Cresskill, NJ: Hampton Press.

Trifonas, P. P. (Ed.). (2003). *Pedagogies of difference: Rethinking education for social change*. New York, NY: RoutledgeFalmer.

Ullucci, K. (2011). Learning to see: The development of race and class consciousness in white teachers. *Race, Ethnicity, and Education, 14*(4), 561–577. Retrieved from http://dx.doi.org/10.1080/13613324.2010.519982

Valencia, R. R. (2010). *Dismantling contemporary deficit thinking: Educational thought and practice*. San Francisco, CA: Jossey-Bass.

Webb-Johnson, G. (2002). Are schools ready for Joshua? Dimensions of African-American culture among students identified as having behavioral/emotional disorders. *Qualitative Studies in Education, 15*(6), 653–671. Retrieved from http://dx.doi.org/10.1080/0951839022000014367

Woodson, C. G. (2000). *The mis-education of the negro*. Chicago, IL: African American Images. (Original work published 1933)

Yosso, T. (2005). Whose culture has capital? A critical race theory discussion of community cultural wealth. *Race Ethnicity and Education, 8*(1), 69–91. Retrieved from http://dx.doi.org/10.1080/1361332052000341006

Zumwalt, K., & Craig, E. (2008). Who is teaching? Does it matter? In M. C. Smith, F. Nemieser, J. D. McIntyre, & K. E. Demers (Eds.), *Handbook of research on teacher education: Enduring questions in changing context* (pp. 404–423). New York, NY: Routledge.

SAAD ALAHMARI

5. OVERCOMING CULTURAL BARRIERS

Reflection of a Saudi Arabian International Student in the United States

The Kingdom of Saudi Arabia (see Figure 1) has experienced tension between tradition and Westernization over the past three decades. Still, Saudi Arabia has managed to maintain a balance between conservative Islamic values, cultural norms, and Westernization. Today, the Saudi education system in all grades provides suitable instructional curricula in diverse fields of arts and sciences, while Islamic instruction remains at its core. This balance helps the Kingdom of Saudi Arabia prepare its citizens for life and work in a global economy.

Figure 1. Map of Saudi Arabia
Permission is granted to copy, distribute and/or modify this document under the terms of the GNU Free Documentation License, Version 1.2

FROM THE KINGDOM OF SAUDI ARABIA TO THE UNITED STATES OF AMERICA

In 2010, I started my journey as an international student in the United States. I was pursuing my M.B.A. at the University of Scranton. At first,

N. D. Hartlep & B. O. Hensley (Eds.), Critical Storytelling in Uncritical Times, 37–41.

I faced issues in dealing with the new academic life in the United States. Two interrelated difficulties I experienced were my English proficiency and the new challenge of interacting in business school in the U.S. A common challenge for international students in higher education stems from having to cope while learning and studying in a foreign language, along with the stressors of full-time enrollment requirements and expectations (*cf.* Li, Fox, & Almarza, 2007).

I was fearful of my accent, which impeded my participation in the class. The source of my anxiety was my pronunciation of some English words, and it became worse when classmates asked me to repeat myself. Another reason I preferred not to participate in class was cultural difference. I didn't want to say anything that might hurt the feelings of my peers or be taken as impolite. However, an inner voice kept telling me that I would not learn more unless I faced these obstacles.

I was encouraged by my faith and my belief that nothing is impossible. I also found encouragement from the university environment. Being a graduate student in the United States was an attractive lifestyle for me. My life consisted of books, attending conferences, and enjoying campus events. This was not the case when I was a student in Saudi Arabia. Compared to the U.S., I felt that being a university student in Saudi Arabia was a job.

The United States and the Kingdom of Saudi Arabia have many differences in their educational systems. For example, education in Saudi Arabia is free for all students at schools, universities, and institutes. In addition, undergraduate and graduate students receive a monthly stipend to help them buy books and to encourage study. However, the Saudi Arabian educational system has restrictive and conservative laws. One of these laws is that students are not allowed to share their thoughts about religion, sex, and/or politics. Another policy is separating girls from boys in schools entirely. The first time I had female classmates was in the U.S., causing me to notice the lack of cultural foundations in the Saudi Arabian educational system. I began to see how my male Saudi peers lacked cultural knowledge about women.

Gender is not the only facet of cultural understanding that goes unexplored in Saudi schools. Compared to the U.S.—which is heterogeneous and multicultural in many places—Saudi people largely belong to the same religion and share the same cultural experiences, ethnicity, and race. These differences create a vastly different educational experience for Saudi and American students. Many educators in the U.S. are expected to teach lessons and address difficulties in social justice in their classrooms with their students. Teachers in early childhood education programs play a pivotal role in addressing issues of culture and diversity. These educators support children's development by instilling in them the tools they need to live together respectfully and stand up to prejudice (Ponciano & Shabazian, 2012).

I believe multicultural education is important; students learn that everyone has special characteristics that make them unique, and they don't have to follow the stereotyped roles society portends. As a Saudi international student studying in American universities, I have seen how engaging with different cultures can positively enhance interpersonal skills. These skills will be helpful when I return to Saudi Arabia with the goal of fostering understanding and acceptance of other cultures among my fellow compatriots. My hope is that they will serve as catalysts for societal change in Saudi Arabia (in terms of accepting other cultures and benefiting from them). Saudi students who study abroad have the opportunity to gain diverse worldviews and return home with this knowledge—one of the objectives of the King Abdullah Foreign Scholarship Program.[1] This potential reality is reflected in Shaw's (2010) study. She found that her Saudi Arabian participants wanted to complete their studies and return home in order to contribute to making Saudi Arabia a better place.

An aspect I find appealing in American universities is classroom discussion and how professors create informal opportunities for dialogue about social and political issues. This dialogical structuring helps students explore a diversity of perspectives, and leads to greater student understanding of the topic under study. It also allows them to hear the thoughts and ideas of other members of the class. Furthermore, open discussion in the classroom prepares students to represent democratic society: "Education is significantly more than information transmission and skill building. It is also very important a developmental process both for student and instructor" (Hubbel & Hubbel, 2010, p. 351).

During my experience studying in the United States, I have made friends from different backgrounds—especially international students at my school—as they have similar academic and personal issues in terms of studying abroad in the U.S.[2]

YET, SOME DIFFICULTIES CONTINUE

Language and culture are not the only obstacles I faced during my first year in the United States. I also struggled with personal challenges, such as homesickness, social anxiety, financial constraints, living arrangements, immigration regulations, and interpersonal relationships. The stresses of these new dynamics were heightened because as an international student I faced invisible pressure as a representative of Saudi students and other international students.

I have been a volunteer in campus events, and I have felt that my adjustment as an international student was developed. However, my off-campus life was still affected by homesickness and linguistic loneliness. The "American" way of living, in general, is extremely different from Saudi life. The main differences are the panoply of religion, language, customs, and traditions. Even though I initially experienced culture shock, I continue to find American higher education to be diverse; I have learned to live with American pluralism and multiculturalism. This acceptance was my solace and eased my transition living as a Saudi international student in the United States. Isolation and longing for home were part of my international student reality; however, I overcame them by volunteering on campus and taking opportunities to talk and learn from students and faculty.

I have grown and continue to benefit from living and learning within disparate higher education systems (U.S. and Saudi Arabia). My journey in American higher education has serendipitously led to me finding my "voice," a process that has also led to greater understanding of multiple cultures. I hope to use my developing knowledge and international student experience to address the tension that exists between traditional and restrictive Saudi perspectives and Western worldviews. Cultural Foundations of Education can facilitate this change.

NOTES

[1] The King Abdullah Scholarship Program (KASP) started in 2005 with an agreement between King Abdullah and President George W. Bush to increase the number of Saudi students in the United States. Despite its recent launch, KASP is the largest scholarship program in the history of Saudi Arabia. For more details, see http://www.sacm.org/ArabicSACM/pdf/education_web.pdf

[2] A number of researchers have extensively examined the academic and personal issues that international students experience while studying in the United States (Olivas & Lee, 2006; Ward, Bochner, & Furnham, 2008).

REFERENCES

Hubbell, L. H., & Hubbell, K. (2010). When a college class becomes a mob: Coping with student cohorts. *College Student Journal, 44*(2), 340–353. Retrieved June 19, 2014, from https://www.uwstout.edu/learncomm/upload/Hyperbonding-Hubbell_2010.pdf

Li, H., Fox, R. F., & Almarza, D. J., (2007). Strangers in stranger lands: Language, learning, culture. *International Journal of Progressive Education*, *3*(1), 1–44. Retrieved from http://dx.doi.org/10.1007/978-3-642-20201-8_20

Olivas, M., & Lee, C. (2006). Understanding stressors of international students in higher education: What college counselors and personnel need to know. *Journal of Instructional Psychology*, *33*(3), 217–222.

Ponciano, L., & Shabazian, A. (2012). Interculturalism: Addressing diversity in early childhood. *Dimensions of Early Childhood*, *40*(1), 23–30.

Shaw, D. (2010). Bridging differences: Saudi Arabian students reflect on their educational experiences and share success strategies. *Dissertation Abstracts International: Section A. Humanities and Social Sciences*, *71*(4-A), 1192. Retrieved June 19, 2014, from http://hdl.handle.net/1957/13826

Ward, C., Bochner, S., & Furnham, A. (2008). *The psychology of culture shock* (2nd ed.). London, UK: Routledge.

6. JUDGING STORIES

Narrative Value in Scholarships

For nearly a decade I have worked in the development office of a community college. This office has the responsibility of awarding the scholarships created by local private individuals and businesses through the college's foundation. Each year, hundreds of students submit their scholarship applications consisting of three essays from general writing prompts, transcripts from previous academic experience(s), and two letters of recommendation from non-family members. For me, the parts of scholarship applications that are the most moving are the stories student applicants share. Judging scholarship essays is difficult; what merits a "worthy" story? This chapter explores issues and challenges associated with judging stories within scholarship applications.

Scholarship applications contain a variety of numbers and metrics. Beneath each name and student ID number is a student's grade point average (G.P.A.), class rank, and the number of college hours completed. Additionally, there is an evaluation of financial need determined from the Free Application for Federal Student Aid (FAFSA). Most college scholarship applications have essays—which allow student applicants to share their story—to avoid reducing students to a series of numbers. In concert with the various quantitative measures of merit/need used by higher education, essays provide applicants the opportunity to share what they see as important and to choose what stories to disclose in addressing the essay question(s).

In this chapter I define college scholarships as monetary rewards created by private entities (corporations, foundations, clubs, and/or associations) and philanthropists. These scholarships are different from financial aid packages and Pell grants, which are primarily driven by FAFSA formulae and don't require student essays. While many community colleges award private scholarships, there is variability in how they are awarded (e.g., essay prompts and eligibility criteria may be unique). Regardless of the prompts, essays are used to distinguish applicants from one another. While G.P.A., class rank, and/or standardized test scores can categorize applicants *efficiently*, these

N. D. Hartlep & B. O. Hensley (Eds.), Critical Storytelling in Uncritical Times, 43–46.

metrics alone cannot *effectively* distinguish similar applicants from one another. What is the difference between two students who boast a G.P.A. of 3.90?

The act of sharing a personal story for a scholarship essay is a self-reflective and political process. The applicant must select a personal story to share, which may be difficult for students who are used to writing essays about historical figures or other external subjects. Writing about oneself stands in contradistinction to what is frequently asked of students in secondary education—to analyze a topic in a detached and prosaic manner. What does it mean for a student applicant to share *his or her* own story? How does the political fit into the judging of auto-ethnographic experience for these students? Whose stories are most valued (and why)?

Scholarship Essays Are a Limited Benefit for Students

Scholarship essay writing is not a learning experience. No feedback is returned to student applicants. With hundreds of applications to review, providing constructive feedback for each essay is infeasible. Even if a student is selected for a scholarship, they likely will not know what part of their application led the committee to its decision. The scholarship process— from a writing educational experience—is a "black box" experience because a majority of the essays are discarded. They are never catalogued, filed, or accounted for in any other way. This shouldn't be the case for such a personal moment, especially from an institution of higher learning.

Writing a scholarship essay is not cathartic for all students. The politics of selecting a scholarship recipient make the writing exercise one that is *not* rooted in personal exploration, but rather, an act of placating to institutional mores and committee member ideals. The process of judgment is always one of bias and values; in my experience, the power of the applicant's self-reflection is a secondary goal, at best. The student applicants are writing for a third party they will likely never meet. The essays are sent into a "black box" of bureaucracy with the hope financial aid will echo back.

Scholarship Essays: Who Do They Benefit the Most?

In the end, the value of writing benefits more than the scholarship applicant. The scholarship essays provide the Development Office with stories it can share among donors (current and future). Donors are gratified when reading these essays because they become part of the student's story, especially in the case of personally endowed scholarships. For higher education, student essays serve as promotional artifacts: snippets of the essays can be used for marketing and for fostering identification and relationship with the college.

Scholarship essay evaluation and selection varies among committee members. Some members may feel the essay should be well written, which would advantage grammarians and wordsmiths. Meanwhile, other members may look for compelling stories that could best characterize the institution. For example, a community college scholarship panel may be seeking stories of first-generation college students, particularly if the stories align with that institution's value of educational access. This same story may not be valued differently at an Ivy League institution, where professional pedigree, institutional prestige, and familial legacy could be seen as more worthy.

Students who are awarded a scholarship may find that their essay is shared with the private individual(s) or organization(s) that created the scholarship. Sharing is seen as good stewardship, allowing for transparency. It is important for the Development Office to show that the scholarship recipient's story aligns with the values of the scholarship creator(s). To promote an essay that did not espouse the beliefs of the donor would be a dangerous act. However, an equal danger may be when (or if) student essays become co-opted by the institution. These essays may be used to create flawed "poster" students. This is a slippery slope for all colleges. To claim that the awarded scholarship was the defining moment that propelled the student to success may rob the student of his or her own agency.

Scholarship Committees Must Be Deliberate in Their Evaluations

Scholarship programs must be responsible with the personal stories that are shared with them. Committee members should be deliberate in examining how they value the stories they read. If there is an overly critical eye toward writing rules and grammar, what students and what methods of storytelling are being (de)valued?

Another fundamental question decision-makers could ask is the following: *What is the goal of the scholarship program?* If it is solely to reward students who demonstrate the learning goals of their previous academic system(s), this can be accomplished with test scores and other quantitative data attached to a student application. If the goal is otherwise, then the selection committee should appreciate students' stories, not the means in which they are told. In the end, scholarship committees are faced with a difficult task—how to judge one narrative as more awardable than others. Simply ignoring grammatical mistakes does not remove biases that can infiltrate the scholarship selection process. A reader may be seeking a certain narrative, thus closing their minds to stories that don't conform.

Two common narratives that may seduce a committee are the "Horatio Alger" and the "Good Samaritan" stories. In the case of Horatio Alger, the committee may privilege an essay that discusses a student raising him/herself up by his/her own bootstraps. This story would embody the theme of individualistic determination, with the writer fulfilling his/her destiny. This is a dangerous narrative to reward with scholarship funding because it punishes the student who does not have such a story to tell. The "Good Samaritan" narrative in student scholarship storytelling centers on an applicant's community service. Surprisingly, the "Good Samaritan" (promotes the collective) story runs counter to the "Horatio Alger" (promotes the individual) story. Because engaging in community service requires having free time, requesting that applicants write about community service presumes they have time to take on this additional work, thereby privileging some students and disadvantaging others.

In conclusion, it is important to remember that scholarships—by themselves—are not tools of social justice. For every scholarship recipient, there are hundreds of applications. Scholarship selection committees and programs must remain vigilant and understand that it is personal stories (not academic prose) being shared and evaluated. The objectives for many institutions of higher education are to uphold concepts of diversity and social justice. Judging scholarship stories should be seen as an opportunity to practice these values.

CYNDY ALVAREZ

7. ONE UNHEARD VOICE FROM THE SHADOWS

Dear Miss Cyndy:

I don't remember the first time I learned about people being undocumented, or as others call it, being an "Illegal Immigrant" or "Illegal Alien." However, I refused to use those terms within this letter because I have learned that it's de-humanizing and derogatory to refer to a human as being "illegal."

I recall my parents telling me that I could not marry until I was at least 21 years old because I needed to "arreglarles," which translates to "fixing them." Turning 21 was seen as a magic number that would solve my family's current situation of living in the shadows. Adults around me always said that when I turned 21 I would be able to "fix them." At age 21 I would be able to petition my parents to become permanent residents.[1]

As of 2011 there were 11.5 million *undocumented immigrants* living in the United States (Yoshikawa, Kholoptseva, & Suárez-Orozco, 2013), and by March 2012 there were 11.7 million *undocumented individuals* estimated in the United States (Passel, Cohn, & Gonzalez-Barrera, 2013). It was reported that 60% of the undocumented immigrants reside within the following six states: Texas, Florida, New Jersey, California, New York, and Illinois. Most undocumented immigrants originate from Mexico, El Salvador, Honduras, and China (Yoshikawa et al., 2013). Within the U.S. undocumented population, the largest group originates from Mexico; a recent Pew study estimates that 6 million Mexican undocumented immigrants live in the United States (*cf.* Valdes & Rodriguez, 2013).

According to Passel and Cohn (2011), one-third of all children with immigrant parents have at least one undocumented parent (80% of these children are U.S. citizens and 91% are under the age of six). In other words, there are many children who are documented but have at least one undocumented parent (*cf.* Passel & Cohn, 2009). Many research studies and policy debates have focused on undocumented children and/or adults, overlooking the population of 5.5 million documented children with

N. D. Hartlep & B. O. Hensley (Eds.), Critical Storytelling in Uncritical Times, 47–54.

undocumented parents. This trend is upsetting given the estimate that at least one child per classroom will have undocumented parents (Yoshikawa, 2011).

That is *one child per classroom* who will struggle with trying to "blend in" or "camouflage" within the rest of the population. As a school psychologist in training, I have become more sensitive to—and aware of—the diverse needs of students, something our training emphasizes. My interactions in the school system—both as a student and as a trainee—have provided me with the insight that U.S. students with undocumented parents are often unnoticed. I recently met a college student named Emma, for whom I've become a mentor. It was through our mentoring interactions that Emma disclosed the struggles of being a first-generation college student and having undocumented parents.

As a school psychologist trainee, I felt the responsibility to advocate for Emma's rights as a student. I wanted Emma's unique voice to be heard, and to increase others' awareness of this population. I wanted to cast light on humans who are forced to live in the shadows.

I told Emma that by sharing her story she would be helping other students in similar situations to tell their own stories. Emma was hesitant about disclosing her personal story; her parents' status has been kept secret out of fear they will be deported. However, Emma agreed that her family's situation was unique and important to reveal. The U.S. public stands to benefit from this story because they are largely oblivious to the experiences of documented children with undocumented parents. After brainstorming several methods to share Emma's experiences, we came up with the idea that she could write a letter to me; therefore, her identity would be kept confidential and I would represent her unheard voice.

The following is the remaining portion of Emma's letter:

As a child I would experience nightmares of my parents getting deported and not being able to stop things. Often I would wake up crying and begin praying to God to protect my parents. Police officers and authority figures (e.g., politicians, U.S. Immigration and Customs Enforcement) were seen as people who could possibly tear my family apart. Therefore, these individuals and groups weren't trusted. My parents did not impose this mindset on me: society did.

Growing up I was able to observe how my parents tried to do everything possible to be "good" citizens. It was the idea that if we were good citizens, stayed out of trouble, and reported our taxes, our behaviors would facilitate the petition process when I turned 21. My parents lived in the shadows but chose to abide by the rules of the land. They avoided situations that would place them at risk for deportation, which ultimately meant avoiding the police, airports, courts, and immigration services.

There was an obvious fear of becoming separated as a family. Being the oldest child in the household, I became my parents' right hand. Looking back, it's heartbreaking that a family would need to develop an emergency plan and instruct their children at such an early age of what they should do in case of a family separation. Whereas some first-generation undocumented families don't have plans for becoming separated, my parents were realists and always had a plan for the what-if "horrible situation." My parents told me the steps that should be taken in the case of an "emergencia," as my mother referred to it. I knew she was referring to deportation. These instructions were provided to me maybe during early adolescence. Imagine growing up with the fear of authority figures taking your parents, and having to keep an emergency plan. Is this a normal childhood? Do all families in America live this way?

As I got older I realized this was not the case. I acknowledge that other undocumented families live under—or are forced into—worse conditions than mine. I also recognize there are undocumented parents who are supposedly guaranteed every American right because their children are documented. However, the reality is I regularly found myself not being able to access all the resources, rights, and/or freedoms because of my parents' legal situation. Yes, I am an American citizen, but my life is experienced through my parents' undocumented status. I worry about deportation. I worry about not getting access to certain resources. I stress about my parents losing their job(s) and having to step in as the head of the household. These are fears many U.S. citizens don't have to worry about, especially if they have documented parents.

When I applied for financial aid for college, it was such a difficult process because my parents lack a Social Security number (SSN). Keep in mind, my parents have always filed their taxes despite not having an SSN. There is a widespread (mis)conception that undocumented immigrants do not file and pay their taxes, hurting our economy. Instead, undocumented immigrants contribute to the Social Security system while never receiving any benefits. I just read in The New York Times *that the chief actuary of the Social Security Administration claimed undocumented workers have contributed close to 10% ($300 billion) of the Social Security Trust Fund (Goodman, 2014).*

Family Health Insurance? This never existed within my family. Fortunately, my brother and I were eligible for health coverage through the Children's Health Insurance Program (CHIP). However, when we turned 18 we lost health coverage.

49

Traveling? *Impossible. Out of the question. The farthest we ever went as a family was Houston, Texas. I had to venture to new places on my own. I was 18 the first time I flew on an airplane. My parents couldn't drop me off at the airport for fear of Immigration Officers being there. Although my parents weren't able to experience certain things, they've always encouraged me to gain experiences they can't access, such as a higher education.*

College? *I was expected to attend, despite my parents never attending. My father only obtained a sixth-grade education, and my mother finished high school, but college was never an option for her. Accomplishments were never overly rewarded in my family, but were seen as a step towards gaining more accomplishments. I was the first in my family to attend college, and I had to discover the process on my own. My parents couldn't help me move into my dorm. Nor could they help me relocate to a different city. My parents were afraid of traveling long distance because they might be apprehended and deported. Throughout life, I've had to sacrifice my parents' presence for our family's protection.*

Graduate School? *My father provided me with his car; that was as much as they could do. I was accepted into several in-state and out-of-state doctoral programs, but making a decision was stressful. Going out-of-state meant leaving my parents on their own. My main concern was that I'd become their right hand, and being out of state would limit what I could do in case of an* "emergencia." *These were things that graduate students with documented parents did not have to take into consideration. Although it would be hard on my family, I ultimately decided to take the risk and attend out-of-state.*

These are some of the challenges that first-generation documented individuals who have undocumented parents might encounter. Will my parents be able to attend my graduate school commencement? Most likely not.

The Magical Number "21"

My 21st birthday wasn't to celebrate that I could legally drink alcohol; it was a birthday to celebrate the opportunity of "arreglarles a mis papas." *My family couldn't have guessed what would happen next.*

My family went to an immigration lawyer the day after I turned 21. We brought every type of documentation (e.g., birth certificates, tax forms, etc.) we could as proof that I was a U.S. Citizen, attempting to petition for my parents' citizenship.

It was a nerve-racking day, and our family's future hung in the balance. Over 21 years we'd accumulated so much hope for this magical day and were expecting to be able to step out from the shadows together. I had so many dreams and "ilusiónes," such as my father attending culinary school, my parents being able to buy a house, going on family vacations, my mother taking English courses and not having to work anymore, my parents being eligible for drivers' licenses, and—most important—the hope of not having to worry about being separated from my parents.

After visiting several immigration attorneys, they all stated similar things. Since my parents entered the country without a visa, they would face a "time bar" or penalty that required them to go back to their native country and remain there for 10 years. Our situation didn't have a solution due to several legal barriers. Therefore, I could not adjust their status, and so we'd have to continue to live in the shadows. So much hope was placed in the magical number of 21; my family was sad and disappointed.

Although amnesty has been promised for quite some time, our hope doesn't exceed our doubt that it will someday happen. Does the U.S. want to provide a pathway to citizenship for its more than 11.7 million undocumented immigrants? Are government leaders forgetting that many undocumented immigrants have U.S.-born children who are unable to access resources because of their parents' status?

Like myself, children are affected by their parents' work conditions. For example, my father started washing dishes at a restaurant. He has become one of the main cooks after 23 years of working for this restaurant. Because he is undocumented he continues to be underpaid; still, against all odds, he has raised a family of four on an annual income of $30,000. We managed to have the basic necessities, but there wasn't room for luxuries, e.g., health insurance. Relying on my father's income without job security has been nerve-racking for my family. Despite being a hard and dedicated worker for over 23 years, he could get fired at any time without reason.

The only reason he would be fired would be because he lacks an SSN— that "magical" 9-digit number. God forbid this ever occurs, but if it did, I would have to become the head and financial provider of the family. Can I afford to sustain a family of four? Perhaps, but I would have to defer my dreams—which would mean dropping out of graduate school.

Although I am a documented U.S. citizen, my life has been a nightmare. Living with a constant fear that my parents would be taken from me has been painful. Why does the "American Dream" have to be a nightmare for families living in the shadows?

Sincerely,
Emma

REACTIONS TO, AND RESEARCH RELATED TO EMMA'S LETTER

After reading the letter, I grew professionally because I learned about the stresses this overlooked population encounters; I also became aware of the need to advocate for this student population. After engaging the literature (Yoshikawa, Kholoptseva, & Suárez-Orozco, 2013) and analyzing Emma's letter, it was clear that her parents' undocumented status impacted her life. Yoshikawa et al. (2013) propose three mechanisms that explain how a parent's undocumented status affects their documented child's development. These three mechanisms—parent-child separation, access to public programs, and work conditions—were present in Emma's autoethnographic letter.

Children with undocumented parents are faced with the threat of separation from their parents (read: deportation). The consequences of separating a child and parent can "harm a child's learning and emotional development due to disruption in attachment, interruptions in school, and economic losses in the household" (Yoshikawa & Kholoptseva, 2013). A study by Brabeck and Xu (2010) reported that higher vulnerability of detention and deportation are associated with greater negative effects on children's emotional wellbeing and academic performance. Revealing the undocumented status of parents is a risk for the entire family since it makes them vulnerable to being deported.

Emma wrote about having anxiety. Research has identified that documented children with undocumented parents often grow up with higher levels of anxiety: Undocumented parents encounter challenges that impact the development, education, and mental health of their U.S. citizen children (*cf.* Brabeck & Xu, 2010; Delva, Horner, Martinez, Sanders, Lopez, & Doering-White, 2013; Rogerson, 2012; Seo, 2011; Xu & Brabeck, 2012; Yoshikawa & Kalil, 2011; Yoshikawa et al., 2013). Yoshikawa et al. (2013) observe that "U.S. citizen children of documented parents are eligible for many of the means-tested benefits that are offered by the federal government, but undocumented parents face barriers to enrolling their eligible children in these programs" (p. 5). Undocumented parents face many obstacles: a lack of knowledge or information about programs, language barriers, and/or fear of being identified as undocumented.

Undocumented parents who are the first to arrive in the United States without any social support will have limited social networks to inform them about available programs. Language barriers can become an obstacle when having to access or enroll their documented children in public programs. Finally, undocumented parents usually don't enroll their eligible children for fear of being placed on the "radar screens" of authorities, organizers, and government officials. An undocumented parent fears being identified, and many programs often require proof of income, which undocumented parents don't always have. The goal of undocumented individuals is to live in the shadows without calling any attention to themselves.

Xu and Brabeck (2012) find that families with undocumented parents don't access services at the same rate as families with documented parents. However, services are utilized at similar rates when having a Latin@ social network to help them access resources and overcome fear of deportation. Therefore, fear of deportation is highest when undocumented parents lack a social support network, leading to them not accessing services. School psychologists can help by developing social support networks for students and their families, which will lead to increased access for all.

It has also been found that a parent's undocumented status is associated with lower levels of standardized cognitive skills in children as early as two years of age as a result of not being exposed to professional childcare programs (*cf.* Yoshikawa et al., 2013). A child's cognitive development is impacted when s/he lives with parents who work for low wages, are undocumented, and/or lack a social support network. These children, born in the United States, are raised with limited resources all because of legal status.

For myself as a school psychologist in training, familiarity with diverse populations of students is important. Students may outwardly appear to blend with the mainstream population, but in reality, many are living in the shadows. It is possible that a student may be experiencing behavioral, social-emotional, and/or academic difficulties from the stresses of their parents' undocumented status. It is crucial that School Psychologists address the impact the immigration system has on child development. Consequently, shouldn't we become advocates for amnesty and a pathway to citizenship?

NOTE

[1] Opening paragraphs of Emma's letter. Emma is a pseudonym for a female college student.

REFERENCES

Brabeck, K., & Xu, Q (2010). The impacts of detention and deportation on Latino immigrant children and families: A quantitative exploration. *Hispanic Journal of Behavioral Sciences*, *32*(3), 341–361. Retrieved from http://dx.doi.org/10.1177/0739986310374053

Delva, J., Horner, P., Martinez, R., Sanders, L., Lopez, W. D., & Doering-White, J. (2013). Mental health problems of children of undocumented parents in the United State: A hidden crisis. *Journal of Community Positive Practices*, *8*(3), 25–35.

Goodman, H. A. (2014). Illegal immigrants benefit the U.S. economy. *TheHill*. Retrieved June 16, 2014, from http://thehill.com/blogs/congress-blog/foreign-policy/203984-illegal-immigrants-benefit-the-us-economy

Passel, J. S., & Cohn, D. (2009). *A portrait of unauthorized immigrants in the United States* (Report). Washington, DC: Pew Research Center's Hispanic Trends Project. Retrieved June 18, 2014, from http://www.pewhispanic.org/files/reports/107.pdf

Passel, J. S., & Cohn, D. (2011). *Unauthorized immigrant population: National and state trends, 2010* (Report). Washington, DC: Pew Research Center's Hispanic Trends Project. Retrieved June 18, 2014, from http://www.pewhispanic.org/files/reports/133.pdf

Passel, J. S., Cohn, D., & Gonzalez-Barrera, A. (2013). *Population decline of unauthorized immigrants stalls, may have reversed* (Report). Washington, DC: Pew Research Center's Hispanic Trends. Retrieved June 18, 2014, from http://www.pewhispanic.org/2013/09/23/population-decline-of-unauthorized-immigrants-stalls-may-have-reversed/

Rogerson, S. (2012). Unintended and unavoidable: The failure to protect rule and its consequences for undocumented parents and their children. *Family Court Review, 50*(4), 580–593. Retrieved from http://dx.doi.org/10.1111/j.1744-1617.2012.01477.x

Seo, M. J. (2011). Uncertainty of access: U.S. citizen children of undocumented immigrant parents and in-state tuition for higher education. *Columbia Journal of Law & Social Problems, 44*(3), 311–352.

Valdes, G., & Rodriguez, C. (2013). Undocumented immigrant population on the rise in the U.S. *CNN.* Retrieved June 4, 2014, from http://www.cnn.com/2013/09/24/us/undocumented-immigrants-population/

Xu, Q., & Brabeck, K. (2012). Service utilization for Latino children in mixed-status families. *Social Work Research, 36*(3), 209–221.

Yoshikawa, H. (2011). *Immigrants raising citizens: Undocumented parents and their young children.* New York, NY: Russell Sage Foundation.

Yoshikawa, H., & Kalil, A. (2011). The effects of parental undocumented status on the developmental contexts of young children in immigrant families. *Child Development Perspectives, 5*(4), 291–297. Retrieved from http://dx.doi.org/10.1111/j.1750-8606.2011.00204.x

Yoshikawa, H., & Kholoptseva, J. (2013). *Unauthorized immigrants parents and their children's development: A summary of the evidence.* Washington, DC: Migration Policy Institute. Retrieved from http://www.migrationpolicy.org/sites/default/files/publications/COI-Yoshikawa.pdf

Yoshikawa, H., Kholoptseva, J., & Suárez-Orozco, C. (2013). The role of public policies and community-based organization in the developmental consequences of parental undocumented status. *Social Policy Report, 27*(3), 1–24. Retrieved July 12, 2014, from http://www.srcd.org/sites/default/files/documents/spr_27_3.pdf

TUWANA T. WINGFIELD

8. ACADEMIC HAZING

A Reflection of My First Year Teaching at a
Predominantly White Institution

...I felt that I had the honor of the whole African race upon my
shoulders. I felt that, should I fail, it would be ascribed to [the] fact that
I was colored...

Fanny Jackson Coppin (paraphrased in Lerner, 1972, p. 89)

INTRODUCTION

African American women are the "cultural assets" to the advancement of the
community and the social agents to educate Black children (Collins, 2001,
p. 34). Historically, African American women have played a significant
role in the education of Black children. Although African American women
have been granted access into the ivory tower, they continue to experience
racism, sexism, and classism, which ultimately impact their social-emotional
wellbeing (Harris & González, 2012). In this chapter I argue that White
students experience cognitive dissonance when they confront their own
misperceptions of African Americans, especially African American women.
Although substantial scholarship captures the experiences of African
American women in higher education, more is needed that unpacks the
experiences of African American women who teach undergraduate students
in Social Work Education programs. Specifically needed is research that
addresses the preparation of White students who will work with historically
marginalized and disenfranchised populations. Through the use of "life
notes" (Bell-Scott, 1994, p. 13), a form of narrative research, I will share
unique experiences I've had, lessons I've learned, and strategies I've used
to overcome "teaching while Black" (Evans-Winters & Hoff, 2011, p. 466).
Even while I write this piece, I know I'm placing myself in a vulnerable
position: speaking truth to power dynamics I experience as a Black female
in academia.

N. D. Hartlep & B. O. Hensley (Eds.), Critical Storytelling in Uncritical Times, 55–66.

The Oppression of Black Women in Academia

As the social work profession continues to grow, Social Work educators will need to find more culturally responsive ways to address the interlocking oppressions of racism, classism, and sexism that function as barriers to African American women surviving and thriving within higher education. In particular, to adequately prepare White students for the field, Social Work programs need to include the study of institutional racism and White privilege in their curricula (Abrams & Gibson, 2007). This chapter holds implications for theory and practice in the fields of Social Work, Cultural Foundations of Education, and Education Policy Analysis, social work practice, and the recruitment of students into the field.

As an African American woman, I acknowledge and understand that I experience what Gordon (1991) calls a "trilogy of oppression" (p. 2): oppression based upon my race, class, and sex. I write my personal and reflective narrative to share the challenges that I've encountered while teaching at a predominantly White institution (PWI) in the Midwest. Black feminist and educational scholars note that Black women have endured (c) overt racist and sexist attacks that reinforce the existence of institutional barriers toward the pursuit of a just and equitable educational experience (Evans-Winters, 2011; Harris & González, 2012). The academy reflects imperialist White supremacist and patriarchal capitalism (hooks, 2013). The passage of major civil rights legislation may falsely imply that racial progress has been made; however, Black women continue to be oppressed at the micro- and macro-level. Research suggests that African American women—both faculty and students—have been persistently scrutinized and attacked for their intellectual pursuits since gaining access into PWIs of higher learning (Williams, 2007).

Black feminist scholars have documented the experiences of Black women who navigate and resist White supremacy within society and hegemonic PWIs (*cf.* Collins, 1991; hooks, 2000, 2013; Lorde, 1984). The narratives of Black feminist scholars suggest that Black women's minds and bodies continue to be attacked and surveilled. bell hooks (2013) argues that the only way Black women can continue to fight back is by naming what hurts. Naming requires us to speak candidly and openly about our experiences when (en) countering racism, classism, and sexism in White spaces. A consequence of being imprisoned and brutally enslaved, the Black woman "was assigned the mission of promoting the consciousness and practice of resistance" (Davis, 1972, p. 85). It is my hope that by speaking *my truth*, I can add to the scholarship of Black feminist literature on countering racism, power, privilege, and oppression that exists in academia, especially in social work education.

In this chapter I reflect on my first teaching experience in a Social Work Department. My chapter reflects my evolving identity as an educator. My work in the academy can be described as a "ground-zero," where my identity as an African American woman/teacher embodies what Toro-Morn (2010) describes as "paradoxical sites of knowledge and conflict" (p. 69). In short, navigating these sites of multiple consciousness (King, 1988)—African (American) and woman— heightens my sense of awareness of what it means to be a Black woman working in an environment that is institutionally imperialist, White supremacist, patriarchal, racist, classist, and sexist.

Theoretical Framework and Methodology

Black feminist thought is an appropriate theoretical framework to unpack my experience as a Black woman working at a PWI. Moreover, this framework provides a structural critique to tell our stories and interrupt deficit discourses about race, class, gender, and sexual orientation (Collins, 1991). In addition to experiencing prejudice and discrimination, I am burdened for both my Black skin and being female. Black feminist theory centers my experiences working at a PWI.

Research has shown that students and faculty of color experience a "chilly climate" at many PWIs (Jayakumar et al., 2009; Sandler, Silverberg, & Hall, 1996). African American women are caught between the interlocking oppressions of race, class, gender, and Western European hegemonic ideology. In the academy people of color feel the effects of isolation, oppression, discrimination, and racism. The retention rate for Black women in the academy is low because higher education administration, policy, and practices do not support them, leading to disconnection. Those who choose to stay, do so risking their own emotional, physical, and psychological well-being (Esposito, 2011).

As an emerging Black female scholar, I feel it's important to reflect on my experiences as an instructor. I use Dillard's (2010) work—a Black feminist educational scholar who honors people of African ascent and their ways of being and knowing—to speak about my own experiences in the academy. Dillard's (2010, p. 662) "endarkened feminist epistemology" counters Western positivist research paradigms dominant in academe. An endarkened feminist epistemology is rooted in Black feminism and is a way of honoring the historical and cultural contributions of African American women at the intersections of race, class, and gender. Black feminist scholars advocate for research that cultivates researcher-participant relationships, maintaining that scholarly inquiry employing an *emic* lens is valid. An endarkened feminist epistemology is relational, resulting in knowledge production that is contrary to White historical canons.

Dillard draws upon Bell-Scott's notion of "life notes," defining them as "unedited, uncensored, woman talk" (Bell-Scott, 1994, p. 13). Life notes can take shape as written prose, journal entries, music, reflections, and other forms of creative art. Life notes provide a crucial sociocultural context necessary for endarkened feminist epistemological meaning-making. Dillard and Bell-Scott argue that traditional canons of empirical social science research fail to include women of color's voices. This failure has resulted in the lived experiences of African American women appearing in alternative media, such as music, poetry, and literature. Dillard (2010) uses conversations with other African American women leaders and researchers to share their life notes in order to "demystify African American feminist ways of knowing" (p. 664). Using life notes challenges traditional methods of obtaining data for research purposes—a process that traditionally objectifies participants and devalues their lived experience. Endarkened feminist epistemology allows Black women to be who they are, their authentic selves.

Life notes can offer different versions of (her)stories and are useful for unpacking the complexity of the Black woman's experience in knowledge production. This knowledge production disrupts White European epistemologies by considering multiple constructions of reality: the social, historical, political, economic, and cultural. Dillard (2010) is right to point out that there isn't a single best way to analyze narratives. However, life notes offer great potential: they deepen discussions by nuancing how research theorizes the unique experiences of African American women, "situating such knowledge and action in the cultural spaces out of which they rose" (p. 670). Although in this chapter I don't interview African American women in academe, I choose to use life notes to document my journey of learning and "teaching while Black" (Evans-Winters & Hoff, 2011, p. 466).

GUESS WHO SLIPPED UP AND BECAME A TEACHER?

The learning process is something that you can incite, literally incite, like a riot.

Audre Lorde (1984, p. 98)

After practicing social work in various social service agencies and schools in the inner city for ten years, I grew to understand how social work and education intersected. Social workers have the privilege of practicing at the intersection of students' academic and social realities. I wanted to be in a position to help children and families by educating future social workers to act as agents of change for social justice and equity. I applied for and accepted an offer as the Director of Recruitment and Admissions at a four-year public university in the Midwest. A condition of my hire was that I would teach 2–3 courses each academic year. I didn't know what courses I would teach—much less how to teach them—but I was excited nonetheless. I had previous experience providing clinical supervision to graduate-level Social Work students in their field placements, so field education was a logical starting point for me to begin my teaching experience. I agreed to teach the undergraduate senior field seminar during my first year. I remember being scared to stand before my students and teach, given that no one actually taught me *how to teach*. One of my colleagues said, "Remember, you have more experience than they do… you will do fine."

I wanted my students to have a similar experience to what I had when I was in my graduate Social Work Program. My graduate program was rigorous, and the professors had high expectations. My professors were student-centered and created a classroom culture that allowed for healthy debates and critical thought about what we were reading. I sought to create a collaborative learning environment in which students learned primarily from each other. Looking back, I hoped to facilitate classroom discussions that centered my students' and my own lived experiences. Perhaps my expectations were unrealistic for undergraduate students, since many of them were used to being told what and how to think. My experience during the first semester of teaching was unlike anything I'd ever encountered.

A Semester of Resistance and Change

I can still remember the first class meeting. My palms were sweaty, and my heart was racing. All I could think was *Tuwana don't trip over your feet or mispronounce someone's name*. My students' eyes peered at me as if I was the sage on the stage. I introduced myself and then asked each student to introduce him or herself, sharing where he or she was placed and what he or she hoped to learn that year. We first discussed classroom norms, something I'd borrowed from my previous mental health consulting work. The norms were as follows: (1) start and end on time,

(2) come prepared, (3) step up, (4) speak your truth, and (5) be willing to experience discomfort. All the students agreed to the norms. We then discussed the syllabus and class assignments. The first several weeks went well—or so I thought—but then I began to notice a change in how the students interacted with me.

For example, the students were required to keep a field journal documenting their experiences, and I would provide feedback. The intention of my feedback was to get them to think more critically about their experiences in the field, and not to make assumptions about their clients. For every critique that I made, I would always find a way to say something positive or encouraging about what they had done in the field. No matter how encouraging I believed my comments were, the students received my feedback as if I was personally attacking them and was unsympathetic that they were beginning social workers. As a result, they became silent and rarely participated in class discussions or even responded to my e-mails. If they did respond, I felt as if I was an object they were addressing to get what they wanted. Evans-Winters and Hoff (2011) note that as a form of resistance, White students use silence as a weapon, or perform in ways that tolerate faculty of color. I began to feel as if my students were only *tolerating* me and had little respect for me as their instructor or even as a human being.

During class time my students didn't participate in discussions but instead would engage in sidebar conversations. I felt disrespected when they talked over me or questioned my competence. Uncertain about what was creating these classroom dynamics (but feeling like there was more going on), I consulted one of my colleagues about how they'd handle a similar situation. My colleague suggested that I contact the educational training institute on campus to facilitate a mid-term chat.

Mid-term chats provide feedback to faculty on the students' course-specific learning in the following four areas: (a) course aspects that aid learning, (b) course aspects that make learning difficult, (c) suggestions for course improvement, and (d) actions students can take to enhance their learning. The chat is an open forum discussion facilitated by another faculty member not affiliated with the department. The instructor isn't present so students can speak openly and honestly about their course experience. The facilitator asks students about their learning in the areas mentioned above; group consensus in each area is sought. Next, the facilitator records the feedback and delivers a final report to the faculty member.

I didn't know what would come from this chat. Moreover, the mid-term chat placed me in a vulnerable position to receive feedback from my students about my performance as their instructor. To say that I was nervous would be an understatement, but in order to survive my first year of teaching I had to address my students' concern(s). Berry (2005, 2010) discusses the importance of *mutual vulnerability* as a significant factor of *personally-engaged pedagogy*. Speaking candidly about lived experience within the classroom context is vital to such a practice.

In the weeks building up to the chat, I engaged my students in discussions that honored their lived experiences while sharing my own, including when I started out in the field. My commitment to shift the existing power dynamic in the teacher-student relationship was reflected in my turn toward *mutual vulnerability* in the classroom.

AFTER THE STORM

The facilitator—a professor with over 20 years of teaching experience—informed me that he'd never experienced a chat like the one with my students. Their participation was more contentious and tension-filled than he'd expected or experienced in other mid-term chats. He told me, from the standpoint of a colleague, that several of my students displayed significant degrees of immaturity and low levels of professionalism.

His comments presented a significant challenge for me, as it would for any faculty member. The most salient points from the final report were the following: (a) I didn't treat the students equitably; (b) I was too critical; (c) my feedback was unprofessional; and (d) I'd get defensive when faced with criticism or disagreement.

The semester storm's final blow was when one of my students told me in confidence that a few students were questioning whether I was qualified for my position as the Director of Recruitment and Admissions. I couldn't believe what I was hearing; I was so angry and hurt by their actions. The following life note is a poem I wrote to capture my feelings during that moment.

> *Here I stand alone at the intersection of my (pre)destiny*
> *and the unknown*
> *one road is all too familiar ...*
> *I see familiar faces and circumstances;*
> *the other road is unknown, dark, filled with spirits ...*
> *I know which direction I'm going to take,*
> *I was prepared for this since before I was born.*
> *Each step I take, the shackles of my oppression drop,*

one, my race...Black
two, my class...middle class (or so I've been told)
three, my sex...woman, female, feminist, womanist...
I now feel free to be me...
to be my true, authentic self...
a phenomenal Black woman.
I see my other mothers, my fundi's,[1] and muses...
Tubman, Cooper, Bethune, Wells, Angelou, Lorde, and others...
all greet me as I take one step closer to my truth...
what felt so unfamiliar and dark became familiar and endarkened...
No longer was I afraid of what could come to pass...
I now had enough courage and strength to take this journey,
on the shoulders of MY fairy god mothers towards the path of
liberation...
Here, I am not alone...

My poem reflects the fear and strength I found to deal with what was once unknown, now known. Black women before me had to endure far greater hardships than I was experiencing. I knew I could draw on their strength and musings to deal with my students. The truth, or their truth, was out. Now I needed to prepare myself to address their concerns. As Lorde (1984) mentions in *Sister Outsider*, the learning process is like inciting a riot, and a riot is exactly what played out during the chat and subsequent discussion.

UNPACKING THE MEANING BEHIND THE MESSAGE

I chose to make my students' truth transparent by posting their feedback from the chat on the walls around the classroom, like a gallery. I opened the discussion by stating it was my understanding that they had a lively chat, and as such, I requested they take time to read the comments and elaborate on their concerns. Initially the students were hesitant to walk around the room, but then, one by one, each got up, walked around, and read the feedback. I advanced the discussion by stating, "So now what...what do we do to change the culture of our classroom?"

There was nowhere for them to run or hide; their words were staring right back at them in black and white, no pun intended. The classroom remained silent until one White male student said, "I don't know what the big fuss is about...you all thought that she was going to be a pushover and she wasn't... so now you need to fess up and take responsibility for what happened."

I wasn't sure how to respond to his statement, but I could tell his words stirred up something for others (who might have been afraid to speak) because I saw a lot of heads nodding in agreement. Next, I asked the students if this was the first time that they had an African American instructor. The class responded with an emphatic "yes!"

I can't say this surprised me. But I was "shocked" that these were students who were preparing to enter the Social Work field. Guiding principles in social work education are the importance of understanding issues of diversity and promoting cultural competence (Council on Social Work Education, 2008). Even if I *had* been their first Black instructor, hadn't they broached the topic of cultural competence in their previous courses?

Confronting Whiteness and Cultural Competence

My students and I would be together for the rest of the school year; it was clear that race would continue to be a focal point of the course. So, I did what I felt was best. I plunged headfirst discussing bias, racism, power, privilege, and discrimination. It wasn't easy to do, but certainly had to be done. I asked the students to clarify issues that hindered their learning (e.g., not being treated fairly, being unprofessional, and being too critical). No one could give me concrete examples. When I confronted the students about rumors that I was unqualified to be Director of Recruitment and Admissions, there was silence in the room.

One young female student said, "I feel sorry for you." I asked her why she felt sorry, and she replied that I didn't receive the support needed to do my job.

I responded, "My role and interactions with you (as students) is as your instructor for this seminar, and not as the Director of Recruitment and Admissions. The only thing I want you to be concerned with is my role as your instructor, and you can rest assured that the university conducted an extensive search and hired the most qualified candidate for the position."

My student's statement—"I feel sorry for you"—reflects Solórzano's (1997) observation that minorities in teacher education programs experience racial microaggressions. Reflecting further on her statement, I interpreted this White female student as saying that she felt sorry for me because she felt I was unqualified and needed extra support to do my work. Her remark was infused with racist ideology about African Americans. Without confronting Whiteness, White privilege, and White identity in social work education, deficit thinking continues unchallenged. Culture (in)competence has implications for how soon-to-be social workers will interact with minority clients (Abrams & Gibson, 2007).

That day I learned it's possible to overcome anything that comes my way. My strength and courage can be attributed to my foremothers and sisters of African ascent. Restraint and patience were needed to unpack the racist overtones in my students' comments from the mid-term chat. I knew I had to make the chat a "teachable moment" and salvage rapport with my students because we still had to work together. I didn't alter every student's evaluation of me, but I took responsibility for what happened in my course. I wasn't a teacher when I began, but by the end of the semester, I was. I learned how to teach while being a Black woman.

FINAL THOUGHTS

My efforts to engage students and show concern for both their academic and social-emotional wellbeing would eventually pay off. After the storm passed, students came to meet with me individually to discuss their concerns about the seminar and their classmates. During the one-on-one meetings, it became clear to me that only a few students were dissatisfied with the course. I realized that no matter what I did, some student's perceptions of me would never change. I had to move forward, finding solace in the fact that the majority of the class was willing to engage in critical conversations about issues that would impact the future clients they'd serve.

Despite having worked in the Social Work field for more than ten years, when I began my teaching responsibilities I was scared. I felt a huge weight of responsibility: like I needed to know everything and to teach my students all that I knew. Similar to Lorde (1984), I feared being "found out," that I wasn't a *teacher*, and I represented all African Americans. I needed to be honest with my students—I too was scared.

My presence as an instructor leads to cognitive dissonance for many of my White students. I am conscious of these students' distorted images of African American women in academe. I will continue to counter negative images by centering race, class, power, privilege, and oppression in my course (i.e., readings, media, class discussion, and lecture). I will also continue being intentional about creating an open- and non-judgmental classroom culture so that my students can be engaged and we can both learn vulnerably. Even though I haven't taught field seminar since the spring of 2011, I'll always remember my first class. They taught me to be fearless and unapologetic for being a Black female academic. Their resistance helped me learn how to be a better instructor.

NOTE

[1] According to Payne (1995), a "Fundi [is] the person who passes the best collective knowledge from one generation to the next" (p. 57).

REFERENCES

Abrams, L. S., & Gibson, P. (2007). Teaching notes reframing multicultural education: Teaching White privilege in the social work curriculum. *Journal of Social Work Education*, *43*(1), 147–160. Retrieved from http://dx.doi.org/10.5175/jswe.2007.200500529

Bell-Scott, P. (1994). *Life notes: Personal writings by contemporary Black women*. New York, NY: W.W. Norton & Company.

Berry, T. R. (2005). Black on Black education: Personally engaged pedagogy for/by African American pre-service teachers. *The Urban Review*, *37*(1), 31–48. Retrieved from http://dx.doi.org/10.1007/s11256-005-3560-8

Berry, T. R. (2010). Engaged pedagogy and critical race feminism. *Educational Foundations*, *24*(3–4), 19–26. Retrieved June 22, 2014, from http://files.eric.ed.gov/fulltext/EJ902670.pdf

Collins, A. C. (2001). Black women in the academy: An historical overview. In R. O. Mabokela & A. L. Green (Eds.), *Sisters of the academy: Emergent Black women scholars in higher education* (pp. 29–42). Sterling, VA: Stylus.

Collins, P. H. (1991). *Black feminist thought: Knowledge, consciousness, and the politics of empowerment*. New York, NY: Routledge.

Coppin, F. J. (1869). Training to become an educator. In G. Lerner (Ed.), *Black women in White America: A documentary history* (pp. 88–89). New York, NY: Vintage Books.

Council on Social Work Education. (2008). *Educational and policy accreditation standards*. Alexandria, VA: Author.

Davis, A. (1972). Reflections on the Black woman's role in the community of slaves. *The Massachusetts Review*, *13*(1/2), 81–100. Retrieved June 19, 2014, from http://www.bowdoin.edu/news/events/archives/images/Community%20of%20Slaves.pdf

Dillard, C. B., (2010). The substance of things hoped for, the evidence of things not seen: Examining an endarkened feminist epistemology in educational research and leadership. *Qualitative Studies in Education*, *13*(6), 661–681. Retrieved June 19, 2014, from http://www.sunypress.edu/pdf/61299.pdf

Esposito, J. (2011). Negotiating the gaze and learning the hidden curriculum: A critical race analysis of the embodiment of female students of color at a predominately White institution. *Journal of Critical Education Policy Studies*, *9*(2), 143–164. Retrieved June 20, 2014, from http://jceps.com/PDFs/09-2-09.pdf

Evans-Winters, V. E. (2011). *Teaching Black girls: Resilience in urban classrooms*. New York, NY: Peter Lang.

Evans-Winters, V. E., & Hoff, P. T. (2011). The aesthetics of White racism in pre-service teacher education: A critical race theory perspective. *Race Ethnicity and Education*, *14*(2), 461–479. Retrieved from http://dx.doi.org/10.1080/13613324.2010.548376

Gordon, V. V. (1991). *Black women, feminism, and Black liberation: Which way?*. Chicago, IL: Third World Press.

Harris, A. P., & González, C. G. (2012). Introduction. In G. G. y Muhs, Y. F. Niemann, C. G. González, & A. P. Harris (Eds.), *Presumed incompetent: The intersections of race and class for women in academia* (pp. 1–14). Boulder, CO: University Press of Colorado.

hooks, b. (2000). *Feminist theory: From margin to center*. Cambridge, MA: South End Press.

hooks, b. (2013). *Writing beyond race: Living theory and practice*. New York, NY: Routledge.

Jayakumar, U. M., Howard, T. C., Allen, W. R., & Han, J. C. (2009). Racial privilege in the Professoriate; an explanation of campus climate, retention, and satisfaction. *Journal of Higher Education, 80*(5), 538–563. Retrieved from http://dx.doi.org/10.1353/jhe.0.0063

King, D. K. (1988). Multiple jeopardy, multiple consciousness: The context of a Black ideology. *Signs, 14*(1), 42–72. Retrieved from http://dx.doi.org/10.1086/494491

Lerner, G. (1972). *Black women in White America: A documentary history*. New York, NY: Vintage Books.

Lorde, A. (1984). *Sister outsider: Essays and speeches by Audre Lorde*. Berkeley, CA: The Crossing Press.

Payne, C. M. (1995). Give light and the people will find a way: Ella Baker and teaching as politics. In C. M. Payne & C. S. Strickland (Eds.), *Teach freedom: Education for the liberation in the African-American tradition* (pp. 56–64). New York, NY: Teachers College Press.

Sandler, B. R., Silverberg, L. A., & Hall, R. M. (1996). *The chilly classroom climate: A guide to improve the education of women: Executive summary*. Washington, DC: National Association for Women in Education.

Solórzano, D. G. (1997). Images and words that wound: Critical race theory, racial stereotyping, and teacher education. *Teacher Education Quarterly, 24*(3), 5–19. Retrieved June 20, 2014, from http://www.teqjournal.org/backvols/1997/24_3/1997v24n302.PDF

Toro-Morn, M. I. (2010). Migrations through academia: Reflections of a tenure Latina professor. In C. C. Robinson & P. Clardy (Eds.), *Tedious journeys: Autoethnography by women of color in academe* (pp. 119–145). New York, NY: Peter Lang.

Williams, H. (2007). *Self-taught: African American education in slavery and freedom*. Chapel Hill, NC: University of North Carolina Press.

BRANDON O. HENSLEY

9. WE ARE NOT "CORDWOOD"

Critical Stories and the Two-Tier System in U.S. Higher Education

When we stop thinking and evaluating along the lines of hierarchy and can value rightly all members of a community we are breaking a culture of domination.

bell hooks (2003, p. 37)

…the two-track system in academe does set up two entirely separate, but unequal tiers in which the upper tier, the tenure track, is treated in a vastly superior manner to the lower tier.

Keith Hoeller (2014, p. 122)

We need to say no to the neoliberal fatalism that we are witnessing ... informed by the ethics of the market, an ethics in which a minority makes most profits against the lives of the majority. In other words, those who cannot compete, die.

Paulo Freire and Donaldo Macedo (1999, p. 26)

HIGHER EDUCATION'S NEOLIBERAL INFERNO

In a recent department faculty meeting, an endowed White male professor commented that the majority of students were "cordwood." As an adjunct professor, I found that his comments bothered me. Is it possible he considered adjuncts—the majority of faculty who teach our nation's undergraduate students (Kezar, 2012)—as expendable objects too? *The New Oxford American Dictionary* defines "cordwood" as wood that has been cut into uniform lengths, used especially for fires.

I believe an "inferno" exists in 21st-century higher education. Neoliberalism has engulfed the academy; its blaze threatens to burn American higher education to the ground, and its smoke conceals who gets harmed. What happens when customers (read: students) can pay no longer and low-wage workers (read: adjunct faculty) can take no more?

What happens when the "cordwood" runs out and the smoke clears?

N. D. Hartlep & B. O. Hensley (Eds.), Critical Storytelling in Uncritical Times, 67–78.

One theme in my current research on adjuncts in a neoliberal economy is their prevalent maltreatment—adjuncts are treated differently and subordinate to tenure-track faculty (*cf.* Hensley, 2013, 2014). In this chapter I focus on the interpersonal, intergroup, and institutional relegation of adjunct faculty by using an autoethnographic approach that draws from composite sketches, unstructured interviews, excerpts of conversations, fragments of personal narratives, and multiple sources that document inequity in higher education labor.

My story reflects critical theory—it unmasks the dominance of neoliberalism by cultivating *conscientização*[1] (Freire, 1970, p. 109)—and moves toward social justice for faculty and students across higher education settings. Autoethnographic storytelling empowers me to expose how false charity and "tenurism"—a system of discrimination of academics based on tenure status—are employed to maintain dominance in the two-tier system of faculty inequity (Hoeller, 2014).

"WE APPRECIATE ALL YOUR HARD WORK"

I sit, waiting in a small conference room down the hallway from the Communication Department office on a cloudy Thursday afternoon. The Department Chair summoned me to attend a Communication faculty meeting. My stomach feels queasy. I suspect when my adjunct colleagues arrive, none of us will mention what's on our minds. Is our time up?

I've always thought Room 318 was odd: the long, shiny cherry-wood conference table, rounded at the edges, and the black ergonomic swivel chairs aren't compatible with beat-up grey carpet and chipping white walls. I'm the first to show up for the meeting. I claim a spot at the far corner of the table that faces away from windows that are cut into the angular walls.

"Hey Brandon, how's it goin'?" Dr. A (Department Chair) asks me as she enters the room. After we discuss our levels of busyness, she turns and begins writing numbers and abbreviations on the chalkboard in front of me. At this point we're the only two in the room.

Dr. A is about 5'6" and slim. She is middle-aged and usually dresses in nylon vests with striped, button-down shirts un-tucked and dark jeans. However, today she has opted for a fleece pullover, jeans, and hiking shoes. Her attire, whether formal or informal, matches the casual rapport she has with faculty members and students. She asks people to call her by first name, and always makes time to chat with students who enter her office unannounced.

Dr. A's administrative assistant, Dee, comes into the room and asks if she has met with a student (one of my former Public Speaking students) who is trying to add a Communication major. "What's her G.P.A. again?" Dr. A asks warily, her shoulders slightly sagging as she stops writing on the chalkboard.

"2.30," Dee answers, her voice lowering, awaiting an answer.

Dr. A exhales in such a way that signals to me that she has a pile of things to do. Still facing the board, she lowers her right hand with the chalk, and quietly says, "I'll email her after this."

Since she took over as chair last fall semester, I've noticed that Dr. A exhibits all the symptoms of "having-too-much-on-your-plate" syndrome, a condition afflicting many department chairs because of the nature of their job. I am reminded of Hecht, Higgerson, Gmelch, and Tucker's (1999) survey of the roles and responsibilities department chairs have—too much for one person to do alone. She looks exhausted, bags under her eyes, with an unopened Mountain Dew bottle next to her attaché case on the table.

Once she is done writing, the chalkboard displays the following information:

1429 LA   316 DEP   BOOK ORDERS APRIL 8

CO 200 STATUS

I'd later learn that "LA" stood for "Live Admits," a term used by university administration to mean students (apparently living ones) admitted for the upcoming academic year. "DEP" stood for "Deposits," or students who have formally committed to attending and have paid already ("That's the number that's most important to us," Dr. A said once we were into the meeting. The number wasn't good; it wasn't high enough).

"CO 200" stood for the Public Speaking course. It's a required course. However, with faculty budget cuts announced—and the recent formation of a committee charged with exploring wide scale changes in curricula— gossip spread through the halls about CO200 becoming an elective with other departments doing their own forms of public speaking instruction. This gossip was particularly ominous for my adjunct colleagues and myself, and the mutual feeling of being worried but not wanting to talk about it was palpable when I saw them in the days leading up to the meeting. "How are you?" "Fine" was about as far as we went.

As the meeting time approaches, my colleagues filter in. I realize this is the first time we've met as a full department in my four years of teaching at the university. The chair *has* called meetings for adjuncts only—such as one held at the beginning of the fall semester on implementing video recording software for assessment of students in public speaking—but never in my experience have all part-time and full-time Communication faculty come together. As the clock strikes 4:30 p.m. we are still waiting for Matthew and Trent, the department's only two full-time faculty members, aside from Dr. A.

* * *[2]

Drawing from the work of Reich (1992), Duggan (2003), and Giroux (2005, 2010, 2014), neoliberalism is a dominant ideology of tax-cutting and government-shrinking policies based on the reasoning "that government is [not only] bad, but also that the 'free market' is the best way of addressing ... any social problem" (Clawson & Page, 2011, p. 6). Critics of neoliberalism argue it has contributed to an embedded banking model of education—to borrow from Freire's (1970) conceptualization—and reproduces harsh inequity and oppression vis-à-vis the expansive hiring of part-time workers. Several authors, including Hoeller (2014), write of the "Wal-Martization" of higher education. Corporatizing education diminishes student learning and weakens education because resources are diverted from authentic learning in favor of rankings, corporate research interests, and athletics (Keeling & Hersh, 2012). The neoliberal banking orientation treats students as faceless customers who buy degrees and faculty as cogs in an assembly line.

The scourge of neoliberalism is spreading throughout higher education. It undermines critical perspectives and enacts (c)overt forms of discipline and control through the use of market-driven practices and rhetoric of "choice" in a supposed free enterprise. For Giroux (2010), "Not only does neoliberalism undermine civic education and public values and confuse education with training, it also treats knowledge as a product, promoting a *neoliberal logic* that makes no distinction between schools and restaurants" (p. 186, italics added).

According to a 2012 survey by the Coalition on the Academic Workforce (CAW), the total number of contingent faculty members—this includes adjunct/part-time faculty, full-time non-tenure-track faculty, and graduate teaching assistants—is 1.3 million and rising. This number accounts for an estimated 75.5% of the instructional workforce in two- and four-year degree-granting institutions.[3] The most current American Association of University Professors (AAUP) estimates indicate the number of part-time faculty has grown by more than 300% over the past 35 years (*cf.* Curtis & Thornton, 2013).

Hoeller (2014) draws attention to the working circumstances of many contingent faculty members, especially those who are on semester-to-semester contracts at several schools only "to eke out the financial existence offered to fast-food workers" (pp. 2–3). The CAW (2012) report estimates the median pay for a standard three-credit course to be $2,700. Therefore, if an adjunct wishes to remain gainfully employed, s/he must be willing to accept every course s/he can find—a teaching burden that usually exceeds a 4/4 load.

My first job offer was for a meager $1,400: I'd be teaching a three-credit course at a college I'd cross a time zone to get to.[4] Because I was offered a second job, I wasn't forced to drive such a long distance. I would've never guessed that four years later my teaching load would be reduced to two classes per semester and the topic of my dissertation would be the experiences of adjuncts.

BACK TO THE DEPARTMENT MEETING

As my iPhone strikes 4:32 p.m. the chatter continues among adjuncts and Dr. A. We can't start until the full-time faculty arrive. I ask if anyone plans to see the Theatre Department production of *Legally Blonde* over the weekend, and Cindy, one of the adjunct faculty, excitedly says, "Yes, I have several students in it and I can't wait to see their hard work!"

"I have some students in it too. One of them is stage manager," I offer, attempting to match her enthusiasm, but the conversation quickly dies off. We try to revive conversation one or two more times, but eventually take to checking our phones. I pretend to be writing in my notebook.

Matthew walks in a few long minutes later (4:36 p.m. to be exact; I checked) and says jokingly, "I went downstairs for coffee and ended up with conversation." Matthew is a lively Assistant Professor of Communication, often speaking emphatically in the classroom. But the energy he displays in the classroom is fleeting when other faculty members attempt to talk with him. Matthew sits down across from me and swivels his chair around to face Dr. A and the chalkboard. He doesn't say anything else for the rest of the meeting.

It's 4:39 p.m. before we decide to start the meeting without Trent, a Full Professor and Endowed Faculty member in the Communication Department. Dr. A thanks us for coming. She says, "We value all your hard work for the department, and I appreciate you setting aside the time for this meeting.

While we're waiting for Trent, let's start with book orders." She reminds us of the due date.

Dr. A reiterates that faculty members' time and teaching skills are valued in the department, just as Trent stumbles in with a yellow notepad under his arm and a smirk on his face. He mumbles, "My apologies," and sits next to Matthew. Trent's hair and graying beard are unkempt. Even though it's a cold and rainy day, he's wearing an orange madras short-sleeved shirt and khaki cargo shorts, and his white feet are exposed by a worn pair of Birkenstocks.

Dr. A asks if there are any questions. None are voiced. She directs our attention to the chalkboard and begins discussing the figures, explaining the numbers and the enrollment situation. While I'm taking notes on "Live Admits" and "Deposits," I hear her use the business term "Leveraging Synergy" (with conviction, but lacking explanation) and how it's needed to make the Communication Department stronger and more visible.

"Decreasing tracks" in the department and "doing what we're best at; more depth, less breadth" are some of the issues Dr. A discusses. She explains that she has met with the Dean of Arts and Sciences and has had extensive talks with Trent and Matthew about the future of the oral communication requirement and "where *we* want to go as a department."

Trent nods in agreement, leaning back in his chair with his hands resting on his stomach. He clears his throat, sits up, and projects: "One of the things we have to figure out as a department is what we're *not*." He allows for a pregnant pause, and then launches into a jeremiad on what he's heard from colleagues who sit on Faculty Senate, namely that the department accepts too many "bottom-thirty" students and that a G.P.A. limit higher than 2.50 should be imposed.

"This would keep out the cordwood," Trent says matter-of-factly, quoting something from an ancient Greek rhetorician before ending his speech with, "We can't be *too* selective though; we still need cordwood to keep things running." His tone is smug and cocksure as he compares underperforming students to cordwood all while smiling and appearing to be pleased with himself.[5]

Dr. A shifts the conversation to the Council on Curriculum, stating that it will study faculty recommendations and make the final decision on the Public Speaking course requirement. "So this brings us to the status of CO 200. Nothing concrete has been decided yet…"

I raise my hand and ask if there are adjuncts on the Council. Dr. A answers, "No. There's one student representative and the rest are full-time faculty." I nod to indicate I won't be pushing the issue.

Trent butts in, "Just to be clear, you all still have your jobs for next fall. If I was a 'betting man' I wouldn't have been so sure a few weeks ago." He emphasizes the glacial pace of faculty deliberation and administrative bungling and concludes, "It looks like the Council is at a standstill until the summer." He leans back in his chair and looks across the table where most of the adjuncts are sitting. His superficial smile suggests he's fighting administration for faculty, but it appears to be forced and not genuine.

A female adjunct in her forties with two kids chimes in, "That's *such a relief*. I was afraid I'd be looking for jobs this spring."

"Nope," Trent replies proudly. "In fact, when all is said and done, we might see *very few changes*."

Trent, the elder statesman, has spoken. Dr. A moves to adjourn the meeting and for the third time says, "We value all your hard work."

DISCUSSION

My fragmented story points to "a culture marked by fear, surveillance, and economic deprivation" (Giroux, 2005, p. 12). As I mentioned in the opening of this chapter, I believe an "inferno" exists in 21st-century higher education. By adhering to neoliberal logic, the inferno is kept burning. The vestiges of neoliberalism (Giroux, 2014, 2005; Reich, 1992) alluded to in my story treat both students and adjuncts as commoditized cordwood—needed to an extent but mostly expendable.

The sentimental phrase "We appreciate all your hard work for the department" speaks to Freire's (1970) concept of *false charity*, while Dr. A's repeated statements can be read as being on the part of the oppressor (or an agent working with/in an oppressive system) to appear benevolent and to keep the oppressed compliant and docile. The repeated use of "we" advances rhetoric of inclusiveness, even though adjuncts were not invited to serve on Council.

Dr. A's platitudes steeped in false charity can be juxtaposed to Trent's condescending arguments for making the Communication major more exclusive. He wishes aloud that "bottom-thirty" students (below 2.50 G.P.A.) would stop being admitted to the program. Likening students to cheap firewood, Trent dehumanizes them; in the process, they become objects and commodities—"Live Admits" and "Deposits"—rather than student learners.

Trent's benevolent oppression can also be seen when and how he spoke up to inform the adjuncts they still had their jobs for the fall (which I took to mean the teaching assignments we already worked out for the fall schedule). False empathy is exemplified here, as Trent, again, invokes "we" as if there's a faculty/administration battle that he's on the right side of. Adjuncts are led to believe that, thanks to Trent's heroics in parliamentary debate, the issue of the oral communication requirement has stalled, and our jobs (read: semester contracts) are safe for the time being.

Trent's prediction—"we might see *very few changes*"—may have comforted some in the room (no big changes = no jobs lost). His seemingly positive announcement could be read as a mechanism for keeping things the way they are, what Hoeller (2014) calls the academic labor system of faculty apartheid (p. 116). Trent's rhetoric and neoliberal logic position change as bad and the *status quo* as good, especially if it means a contract in the fall.

Hoeller's (2014) work on tenurism describes the term as a dominator system (similar to rankism) in which teachers are categorized based on their tenure status. Tenurism is built on the false assumption that tenure (or non-tenure designation) defines the quality of a professor and justifies his/her place in the higher education system. Tenured/non-tenured binaries fuel the oppressive conditions adjuncts work under. Despite Dr. A's rhetoric—"We appreciate all your hard work for the department"—echoed throughout the meeting, the two-tier (tenured/non-tenured) system only reinforces oppressor/oppressed relations.

By remaining silent after Dr. A answered my question about adjunct representation, I performed docile compliance. Why didn't I push back? Why didn't I stand up for one of my former students who would later be excluded from the major because of her G.P.A.? Why did I remain silent while an endowed professor chopped down students as cordwood?

These questions make me uncomfortable because they force me to look deep into my soul. I know why I stayed quiet. I kept my mouth shut for economic and professional reasons: I aspire to become a tenure-track professor and in order for me to do that I need to complete my doctorate while paying my bills. In short, I needed the next contract. I keep telling myself that if I keep "behaving" that some day I'll land a tenure-track position. I perpetuated adjunct oppression to stay employed and keep my dream alive.

I don't take my (in)actions lightly and have since reflected on my choices. I wrote a poem:

I have sacrificed my critical soul for the illusion of being appreciated,
thinking this would lead to full-time employment or at least
a contract that can minimally sustain my school and living expenses.
Yes, I am "appreciated" at my university but not valued;
I am cordwood cut to two courses for the upcoming semester.

A week before the faculty meeting, Dee, the administrative
assistant, told me
"there's nothing we can do" when I asked about getting a third class.
I need three classes just to stay afloat with rent/debt/food.
I played it cool after hearing the bad news, not wanting to
hint how desperate
the situation was/is. "I will try to pick up a class at the
community college," I said, performing
detached calmness on the outside, though the inside was/is burning.
I am cordwood, cut to the core, left wanting more.

CONCLUSION

The details I choose to share in my autoethnographic story are filtered through the experiences, values, and biases I bring to the process of remembering and writing the meeting. I acknowledge the incompleteness of my interpretation, and make no claims to be objective in how I depict people or events. Critical storytelling can be used to alarm automatons[6] inside and outside American higher education of the inferno. Hollow praise from tenured faculty feeds the flames of neoliberalism and doesn't lead to positive change, equity, or inclusion; rather, it serves to perpetuate the problem.

By sharing my lived experience and reflexivity—laying bare my motives and complicity—I begin the work of "unhooking" (Hayes & Hartlep, 2013) from systems of domination such as neoliberalism and tenurism, which maintain an imbalance of power in higher education. In the last thirty years, adjunct faculty have become the subjugated "other" within higher education's tenure sytem: those who have tenure or are working toward it, and those who are non-tenure-track, or adjunct. The two-tier faculty system reinforces disparities in employment conditions, promotion, and job security, while relying heavily on "non-tenure-track" faculty.

The hierarchy is reified in invisible ways that prospective students and families touring the campus do not see. Unlike tenured/tenure-line faculty, adjuncts are unable to access many opportunities.[7] Hoeller (2014) argues, adjuncts' insidious exploitation often appears to be business as usual— teachers are still rushing to class and students are still sitting in classrooms, taking tests, and working toward graduation. Because neoliberal logic conceals power relations within higher education, counterstories are needed to correct misunderstanding.

Storying adjunct faculty members' lived experience using multimedia is one step toward disrupting acts of adjunct oppression in academic settings—i.e., false charity and benevolent pronouncements that adjuncts can keep their jobs. This storytelling will require more counternarrators to make these acts known on a grand scale, where collective resistance can weaken the system of "faculty apartheid" (*cf.* Hoeller, 2014).

By examining the ways that working conditions for adjuncts are oppressive, higher education faculty (and administrators), justice-oriented activists, and policymakers can gain nuanced understandings of the struggles adjuncts face while carrying out the important work of educating 21st-century students. As more critical stories are told, read, and heard, change may emerge within institutions of higher education. To extinguish the neoliberal inferno, social justice needs to be placed at the center of higher education policy and practice.

Adjuncts make up more than half of the professorial workforce, and the everyday teaching of undergraduates in required courses largely depends on their labor (Kezar, 2012). Excluding adjuncts from making decisions is not justice-oriented, and supports neoliberal policy and practice. Hoeller (2014) admonishes the neoliberal university when he points out that "[t]he contingent faculty movement is a civil and human rights movement. Higher education is not simply another commodity produced by American factories" (p. 151). I agree with Hoeller and submit there is a real need for critical storytelling and research for garnering attention to the ivory tower being on fire. Hope may be found in the growing number of voices calling for higher education to address the discrimination and oppression of its contingent faculty. The time has come for direct action; adjuncts and students are not cordwood.

NOTES

[1] Paulo Freire writes of *conscientização* as critical consciousness, a way of living that involves deeply examining self perceptions and biases, questioning master narratives of history, and acting against forms of oppression when becoming aware of their operation. As Freire (1970) writes in *Pedagogy of the Oppressed*, "Critical reflection is also action" (p. 128).

[2] Note to readers: Similar to what was used in Hartlep's Chapter 2, these asterisks (* * *) indicate time has passed or a shift in thought has occurred.

[3] The CAW authors draw this estimate from U.S. Department of Education data.

[4] I was living in Illinois but had to travel to Indiana.

[5] I looked up definitions of "cordwood" and found it is expendable firewood cut into uniform lengths.

[6] In *Pedagogy of the Oppressed* Paulo Freire (1970) builds on the thoughts of Erich Fromm: "It is essential for the oppressed to realize that when they accept the struggle for humanization they also accept, from that moment, their total responsibility for the

struggle. They must realize that they are fighting not merely for freedom from hunger, but for freedom to create and to construct, to wonder and to venture. Such freedom requires that the individual be active and responsible, not a slave or a well-fed cog in the machine. It is not enough that men are not slaves; if social conditions further the existence of *automatons*, the result will not be love of life, but love of death" (p. 68, italics added).

[7] By opportunities, I'm referring to representation, promotion, and benefits.

REFERENCES

Clawson, D., & Page, M. (2011). *The future of higher education.* New York, NY: Routledge. Retrieved from http://dx.doi.org/10.4324/9780203834183

Coalition on the Academic Workforce (CAW). (2012). *A portrait of part-time faculty members.* Retrieved June 4, 2014, from http://www.academicworkforce.org/CAW_portrait_2012.pdf

Cordwood. (n.d.). *The new Oxford American dictionary.* Cupertino, CA: Apple, Inc.

Curtis, J. W., & Thornton, S. (2013). The annual report on the economic status of the profession 2012–13. *American association of university professors.* Retrieved June 4, 2014, from http://www.aaup.org/file/2012-13Economic-Status-Report.pdf

Duggan, L. (2003). *The twilight of equality? Neoliberalism, cultural politics, and the attack on democracy.* Boston, MA: Beacon Press.

Freire, P. (1970/2000). *Pedagogy of the oppressed* (30th anniversary ed., M. B. Ramos, Trans.). New York, NY: Continuum. (Original work published 1970)

Freire, P., & Macedo, D. (1999). *Ideology matters.* Lanham, MD: Rowman & Littlefield.

Giroux, H. A. (2005). The terror of neoliberalism: Rethinking the significance of cultural politics. *College Literature, 32*(1), 1–19. Retrieved from http://dx.doi.org/10.1353/lit.2005.0006

Giroux, H. A. (2010). Bare pedagogy and the scourge of neoliberalism: Rethinking higher education as a democratic public sphere. *The Educational Forum, 74*(3), 184–196. Retrieved from http://dx.doi.org/10.1080/00131725.2010.483897

Giroux, H. A. (2014). *Neoliberalism's war on higher education.* Chicago, IL: Haymarket Books.

Hayes, C., & Hartlep, N. D. (Eds.). (2013). *Unhooking from whiteness: The key to dismantling racism in the United States.* Rotterdam, The Netherlands: Sense Publishers. Retrieved from http://dx.doi.org/10.1007/978-94-6209-377-5

Hecht, I., Higgerson, M., Gmelch, W., & Tucker, A. (1999). Roles and responsibilities of department chairs. *The department chair as academic leader.* Phoenix, AZ: ACE Oryx. Retrieved from http://dx.doi.org/10.2307/2649267

Hensley, B. O. (2013). The absent adjunct. *The Adjunct Project.* Retrieved June 14, 2014, from http://www.adjunctproject.com/the-absent-adjunct/

Hensley, B. O. (2014). How far from income equity are faculty in four-year, non-doctoral universities? *Journal of Academic Administration in Higher Education, 10*(1), 13–18.

Hoeller, K. (2014). (Ed.). *Equality for contingent faculty: Overcoming the two-tier system.* Nashville, TN: Vanderbilt University Press.

hooks, b. (2003). *Teaching community: A pedagogy of hope.* New York, NY: Routledge.

Keeling, R. P., & Hersh, R. H. (2012). *We're losing our minds: Rethinking American higher education.* New York, NY: Palgrave Macmillan.

Kezar, A. (Ed.). (2012). *Embracing non-tenure track faculty: Changing campuses for the new faculty majority.* New York, NY: Routledge.

Reich, R. B. (1992). *The work of nations: Preparing ourselves for 21st-century capitalism.* New York, NY: Vintage Books.

U.S. House Committee on Education and the Workforce Democratic Staff. (2014, January). *The just-in-time professor: A staff report summarizing eForum responses on the working conditions of contingent faculty in higher education.* Washington, DC: House Committee on Education and the Workforce. Retrieved June 14, 2014, from http://democrats. edworkforce.house.gov/sites/democrats.edworkforce.house.gov/files/documents/1.24.14-AdjunctEforumReport.pdf

MICHAEL CERMAK

10. MR. DOLCE GABBANA

INTRODUCTION[1]

An urban school district in the Midwest wanted to create a new high school with specific career tracks. At the time, I was working at a nearby community college and was tapped by the New Deal Board of Education to help plan and launch the school. Students who applied to New Deal High School were interviewed. I bought new glasses that had a D & G insignia on the temple. Little did I know, the D & G signaled that I was a wealthy white guy who didn't know anything about the students I was interviewing. I learned that John (a man I still keep in touch with) nicknamed me "Mr. Dolce Gabbana."

Fours years later, John was sitting at my kitchen table waiting for me to drive him to college. In this chapter I reflect on my time at New Deal by writing about my memories.

Why a New High School?

Business leaders needed a pipeline of qualified workers. Their demands were getting louder, and the New Deal School District felt pressure to do something. The New Deal Board of Education responded by proposing the start of a new, tech-based high school. The new secondary school would work with local industries and assist students as they transitioned out of high school.

The community of Jonesboro—long a manufacturing stronghold in the Midwest—lost thousands of jobs over the years. Many saw a new high school as a source of new workers and, in turn, a chance to boost the town's economic development. I was charged with the task of getting the school up and running. This role led to meetings with school and community officials. During our talks I stressed my vision of New Deal High School—not to churn out automatons who can be *workers* at the few remaining factories, but to educate students who can be lifelong *learners.*

During site visits to local businesses I heard a similar refrain: "Not every kid will go to college." Although I discussed how the new school could provide

N. D. Hartlep & B. O. Hensley (Eds.), Critical Storytelling in Uncritical Times, 79–84.

students with opportunities to pursue postsecondary education, employers in Jonesboro seemed most concerned with their need for qualified workers (read: high school graduates). Because the support of local businesses was vital to New Deal's future, I needed to balance the needs of employers and students.

I gained traction with Jonesboro businesses when I broached the topic of credentials. At the time I hadn't read Randall Collins's (1979) *The Credentialing Society,* but I did realize New Deal students could benefit from pursuing more than a high school diploma. For Collins, the credential serves as a gateway and allows an individual to secure a position within an organization. Make no mistake about it; I didn't want to fall prey to what Paulo Freire (1970) identifies as the "banking system" of education. In my vision, New Deal would operate in a relational way: knowledge wouldn't be "deposited" into the minds of students for narrow purposes. Rather, New Deal would provide opportunities for its students to make connections with the larger Jonesboro community.

Interviewing Students

Once the New Deal Board approved the school, I had a monumental task; I had less than a year to develop a schedule, recruit students, and hire staff. To top it off, a concerned board member asked me how I would ensure equity in the process of recruitment. My response would be to interview every student who applied. The interview would provide time and space for students to tell me their stories.

I'd like to believe my approach to interviewing was humanizing; however, I suspect students didn't always receive it this way. The interviews took place in a conference room in the Board of Education Building. The strange irony was that several prospective students had been in this building before—the Board of Education is where expelled Jonesboro students and their families attended hearings (making it an uninviting space).

I didn't anticipate receiving detailed responses to my questions about why students were applying to New Deal High School, partly because of the location of the interview and partly because I might've been perceived as an inexperienced principal.[2] In hindsight, I would've conducted student interviews in a more neutral space (not at the Board of Education Building) because of the hierarchical and authoritative nature of the administration building. I also would've had more interviewers present in the room.

First Days

In the days leading up to the opening of the school, I was filled with feelings of anticipation and fear. I couldn't sleep, and I kept thinking, "What am I doing?" I wondered if the buses would run on time and pick students up correctly at stops. My fears dissipated when the first bus arrived. I welcomed students by name as they exited the bus.

Despite being located on a community college campus, New Deal students weren't greeted by college officials on the first day. This was the first hint of the challenges that would come in the school's opening.

Everything seemed to be going as planned during the first week: buses were arriving on time, lunch logistics were working out, and school dismissal wasn't disrupting the college. The only exception being: I regularly joined the students during dismissal. Accompanying students outside of the building would come back to haunt me.

One day I came back into the building only to see one of my students sitting on the ground with his hands handcuffed behind his back. To this day, I don't know all the details, but in my absence a student was disciplined by a campus police officer.

The next day, eight parents were waiting in my office before I arrived. Their faces spoke volumes: they didn't have to utter a word to communicate their frustration. Most of them hoped New Deal would be different from their previous school(s). After all, many of the parents wanted to protect their children from the police-state atmosphere typical in larger urban schools.

One week into the new school year and a student was handcuffed, perhaps without reason. I listened attentively to the eight parents, assuring them this event was an anomaly, not an indication of how the campus community treated New Deal students. While the parents were unsatisfied with my explanation, I believe they trusted what I'd said. They were willing to keep their student(s) enrolled for the time being.

"Open" Campus Lunch

New Deal High School moved into a different building after its inaugural year. Previously an elementary school, our new building was given a fresh coat of paint and new desks. A second cohort of students was interviewed, and the schedule for next year was complete.

New Deal Students reacted with mixed feelings about relocating. Being housed on a college campus made the school unique. Because high school students were used to traditional school environments, the college campus felt liberating. I wanted to ensure the new building was as "open" as it could be.

I wanted students to be able to eat lunch wherever they wished at the new school. The repurposed elementary school had a spacious gymnasium, verdant grounds, and a lab with up-to-date computers.

I overlooked a crucial detail in my scheduling: New Deal staff needed time for lunch, which left me to manage all the students alone. My oversight put New Deal students and staff at risk. Many staff members didn't agree with my plan of making the campus "open" during lunch.

Many teachers believed students should remain in one place so they could be monitored. Students pushed the boundaries, eating lunch in spaces that made monitoring everyone nearly impossible. The teachers who weren't happy gave me a look of "we-told-you-so." These faculty members were so agitated they didn't talk to me for weeks. Taking things into their own hands, they hastily pulled an accordion gate across the hall. Their behavior indicated they were unwilling to let students get acclimated to the "open" lunch policy. I pleaded with New Deal teachers to show faith in the process: be patient with students and they'll eventually self-manage.

Faculty bought into my approach and became less rigid when they saw students behaving in non-threatening ways. Teachers and students played pick-up games of basketball, beanbag toss, and badminton during lunchtime. Students also enjoyed the computer lab and were relieved when I didn't bust them for being on YouTube or Facebook. They'd still instinctively minimize browser windows, but in an attempt to save face they'd poke fun at my glasses, calling me Mr. Dolce Gabbana.

Recognizing My White Privilege

I'll never forget the day I offered to drive Sha Reese home. It was the first time I interrogated my white privilege. As a white male from suburban Chicago, I'd never had to.

Sha Reese—a young Black student—had spent most of the day in the principal's office because she was unable to work with her teacher. Sha Reese sat motionless and expressionless for hours; nothing evoked a response. When the school day ended, she didn't get on the bus. Although it wasn't uncommon for students to stay after school, I was worried—it was getting late.

By 5:00 p.m. the building was closing, and Sha Reese needed to get home. I offered to give her a ride because her mother couldn't pick her up. Sha Reese said she needed to call her mother so she knew when we were leaving. Sha Reese noticed I was nervous about the situation.

She asked me, "How do I know you're not going to dump me on the side of the road?" Her question made me realize I'd been a fool. Here I was, a white man, in a position of power, nonchalantly offering Sha Reese a ride home. With both my hands on the wheel, and sweating profusely (despite the cool weather), I safely dropped off Sha Reese at her home.

While driving to my home after dropping Sha Reese at hers, I recognized my white privilege. As the white Principal of New Deal, I realized my title, race, and authority might intimidate the minority students I claimed to serve. I came to the realization that I could never completely understand why people of color mistrust institutions such as schools. For example, being handcuffed by police and sitting for hours in a principal's office are things I've never experienced myself, but some of my New Deal Students did. I felt horrible because I sold New Deal as something different. Working in a diverse high school left an indelible mark on me, and the experience continues to shape me.

John and Mr. Dolce Gabbana Go to School

Currently I am an Associate Dean of Business at Rolling Meadows Community College. It's hard to believe I've been away from New Deal for over four years. Budget cuts forced New Deal High School to close its doors before it could celebrate a second graduating class. Notwithstanding, I still maintain relationships with former students such as John.

John, the young man who nicknamed me "Mr. Dolce Gabbana," is now a 20-something man who will occasionally text me pictures, like one that displayed his diploma with the caption: "Good times!" He continues to find his way in life, and he seeks me out for career and job advice, for which I am grateful. He asks if I still have those glasses.

When I left my position as a New Deal High School Administrator four years ago, I began working towards my Ph.D. in Higher Education. My doctoral coursework has included studying Cultural Foundations of Education and has been a catalyst for self-reflection. Thinking about my time as principal of New Deal High School, I believe it's possible to overcome mistrust.

NOTES

[1] All names (e.g., people, schools, etc.) in this chapter are pseudonyms.
[2] I was young, new to the district, and a relative unknown to community members. With no history as a teacher in the district like other principals, I was a true outsider as well.

REFERENCES

Collins, R. (1979). *The credential society: An historical sociology of education and stratification.* New York, NY: Academic Press.
Freire, P. (1970). *Pedagogy of the oppressed.* New York, NY: Continuum.

ERIK DALMASSO

11. TAPPING A DRY WELL

A Closer Look at Rural Education Philanthropy

I attended an Enrollment Management Conference at the University of Southern California (USC). Most of the conferees were from Ivy League and elite private institutions. I felt like an outsider because I represented a small public state university. Because I didn't hail from an elite institution, I felt inadequate. The conference title—"Defining Merit: The Nexus of Mission, Excellence, and Diversity"—was misleading to me because of its lack of institutional diversity.

Standardized testing, score reporting, and weighted grades were debated. Many presentations focused on concerns around financial aid and student merit. After the conference was well underway, I had many unanswered questions related to rural education philanthropy—a topic that wasn't found in the program. I wondered why rural students were not included in discussions related to merit and college access. When I returned to my hotel room, I searched for scholarship on rural poverty and college-going patterns of rural high school students. I skipped the exclusive networking mixers and overpriced meals in order to do research. My research interest suddenly became evident.

* * *

I work at a rural (mostly white) university in Central Illinois. The university's admission standards are accommodating, and we admit a higher number of underserved students than most public universities in Illinois. Retention programs, freshman mentoring, and success initiatives are central to the mission of the institution. Although the university has generated rapport with (sub)urban school districts—and worked hard to create opportunities for students who want to attend our institution—it hasn't done enough for rural students in the area.

My advocacy for rural education doesn't stem from an institutional allegiance. Rather, my passion is borne out by my personal experience as a rural, low-income student. Most of my friends were either first-generation

N. D. Hartlep & B. O. Hensley (Eds.), *Critical Storytelling in Uncritical Times*, 85–92.

college students or high school students who entered the workforce after graduating. The pursuit of higher education wasn't seen as the most important thing in one's life.

What stands in the way of rural students going to college? Could it be that rural K–12 students are not being encouraged to attend by their families and teachers? Or is it because college is so expensive? I would submit it could be both.

My doctoral research focuses on how higher education philanthropists can raise funds that rural students in Central Illinois can use to attend college. Funding comes in many forms: monetary donations, scholarships and fellowships, endowed professorships, naming rights, and sponsorships.

* * *

Foundations and Development Offices proliferate in U.S. higher education. As state appropriations decrease, institutions need to supplement their budget shortfalls. This pattern at four-year colleges/universities has continued over the past 30 years. Institutions compete for grant and gift dollars that can slow the rise in tuition costs for their students (*cf.* Goldrick-Rab & Kendall, 2014).

Dwindling state appropriations and institutional competition have made distinctions between who receives (or doesn't receive) funding more stark. Does the school's Carnegie Classification[1] influence the level of philanthropy? Specifically, is it possible for rural colleges to receive more funding in a climate of increased competition and reduction in state dollars?

Development Officers engage donors—potential and otherwise. Drezner (2011) argues the practice of engagement flourishes when a culture is created that emphasizes connection with the university. Students interact in this culture, faculty work in this culture, and alumni appreciate this culture. An institution that has a "culture of giving" is impossible to miss: it's contagious to outside visitors (*cf.* Drezner, 2011). The ability of the college president to articulate mission and vision is essential to cultivating school spirit and philanthropic generosity from outsiders (Elliot, 2006).

A challenge of fundraising is recognizing who can give within pools: alumni, friends, and corporate partners. Drezner (2013) notes, "[N]umerous empirical studies show that a positive relationship exists between a person's level of education and the propensity to engage in pro-social behavior, in particular to donate money" (p. 71). It's important to consider *who* gives because questions of (im)balance are generated.

Drezner (2013) also argues that the alumni pool is too narrow of a "giving community" for meaningful development work. He notes that connecting with current students within a "culture of giving" is effective for building a successful base of donors. Reaching out to local businesses can produce a diverse donor base, while also providing viable connections with graduating students who may soon be employed by these businesses. Relationships and partnerships with industry can provide economic stability for institutions of higher learning and the communities in which they are situated. Along with industry, engaging marginalized communities—including Lesbian, Gay, Bisexual, Transgender, Queer, Intersex, Asexual, and Ally (LGBTQIA), African American, Indigenous, Latin@, Asian/American, women—can provide a diverse base of givers (Drezner, 2013).

Significant barriers remain when engaging a "giving community." It's up to Development Officers to understand donor behavior. Understanding differences in giving and who receives gifts is important. For instance, Elliott (2006) finds that men want to be noticed for their gift, and give without restrictions. Women tend to give gifts that are more long-term, calculated, and anonymous (Elliott, 2006). African-American philanthropists traditionally give to education, religion, and health organizations. Meanwhile, the giving behaviors of the LGBTQIA community are only beginning to be researched (*cf.* Drezner, 2013).

Student need is driving Higher Education Philanthropy as a field. According to Hall (1992), philanthropic giving is the "single force … responsible for the emergence of American higher education" (p. 403). Foderaro's (2011) comments in *The New York Times* are informative and worth being quoted at length:

> As state legislatures cut back support for higher education, public colleges and universities across the country are turning to their alumni, hat in hand, as never before – hiring consultants, hunting down graduates, and mobilizing student phone banks to raise private money in amounts they once thought impossible. But many find themselves arriving late to the game. The rush to catch up has placed public campuses in an awkward stance: cutting academic programs and instructors at the same time they are expanding development staffs and investing in fundraising infrastructure. (p. A1)

* * *

Bekkers and Wiepking (2011) introduce a framework that can be used in philanthropic work. Although Bekkers and Wiepking's model was initially created for the social sciences, it can be employed in higher education environments. The authors offer mechanisms for viewing philanthropy.

Explanation of the Mechanisms. According to Bekkers and Wiepking (2011),

> The categorization of mechanisms is based on the differences in four dimensions, that can be captured by the questions "What?" "Where?" and "Who?" The first dimension is the "what," or the physical form of the mechanism. Is it a tangible object that can be touched? The second dimension is the "where," or the location of the mechanism. Is it located within, outside or between individuals? The third and fourth dimension constitute the "who," or the parties involved. The third dimension is the actor in the mechanism. We distinguish beneficiaries, (charitable, non-profit) organizations, donors and alters (people in the social environments of donors). The fourth dimension is the target of the cause (who is affected). Targets may be donors or beneficiaries. (p. 928)

Bekkers and Wiepking go on to mention,

> Each of the mechanisms is a different combination of values on the four dimensions. [...] [T]he order in which the eight mechanisms are presented do not reflect the importance or causal strength of the mechanism. Rather, the order corresponds to the chronological order in which they affect giving in the typical act of donation. (p. 929)

Considering need. All institutions have needs. Campus infrastructure, scholarships, and deferred maintenance are just some of these needs. Building healthy reserves is also a growing concern given shrinking state appropriations. Determining and ranking the importance of needs (typically resulting in a master plan or strategic plan) is a political process and can take years. Asking for funding is deliberate and calling donors repeatedly can prove counterproductive. Before embarking on a development mission, campus leadership must be clear in its foci.

Since step two can take years (see *Solicitation* below), it's important to engage the correct donor base with an appropriate need. This campus review process is ongoing and fluid. As with anything, needs and timelines change—but major institutional necessities should be made clear to the entire campus population.

Imbalance is present in Bekkers and Wiepking's (2011) first mechanism: community colleges typically identify needs directly related to students, while public four-year institutions often identify major infrastructure projects and foundation reserves as major needs. Some of this imbalance is inherent, as community colleges serve different student populations than four-year institutions.

Solicitation. The "ask." As mentioned earlier, institutions must have a "culture of giving" to be successful at engagement. The engagement of donors can take years of "friendraising" before the actual solicitation can be performed. It's common for institutions to have committed resources in the areas of alumni and development. University Advancement is charged with the solicitation of gifts.

There's a dearth of scholarship examining solicitation of gifts at community colleges. Because of a growing need, the Council for Advancement and Support of Education (CASE) has recently added programming that focuses on solicitation processes at community colleges. Limited research has left community colleges scrambling to put together piecemeal solicitation plans.

Community colleges—whether urban or rural—serve a broad region, making it difficult to build a donor. Although technology has helped in this process, the road to acquiring new funds is long and tedious.

Costs and Benefits. Costs are important to donors. Institutions work hard to ensure the "ask" is appropriate for the donor's capacity to give. If the request is too high, the donor might be turned off; if it's too low, the institution might have lost money (Drezner, 2013). Bekkers and Wiepking (2011) explain that scheduling and location play active roles in donors' willingness to engage in philanthropic discussions. Different solicitation methods also lead to costs. Postal mail solicitations typically result in lower gifts. Direct face-to-face solicitations often yield higher gift amounts (Bekkers & Wiepking, 2011).

"Cost" can mean more than dollars and cents. All donors (regardless of the size of gift) can feel a sense of pride in the campaign or institution. Donor relations should be handled delicately because it's likely the university will request donations again.

Donors want to feel important and appreciated. Many times donors receive benefits according to the size of their gift. For example, donations constituting an "above-average" gift might be rewarded with dinner invitations, executive meetings, or sporting events. Smaller donations are recognized in a yearly foundation summary or on plaques that appear on campus. Again, stewardship is an ongoing process and must be managed carefully and with great detail.

Imbalances of philanthropic giving are reflected in the "costs" incurred by institutions and the "benefits" afforded to donors. The dynamics of donating are unique to each institution. For example, a community college's ability for outreach and stewardship can be limited by staffing (*cf.* Cohen, Brawer, & Kisker, 2013).

Altruism and crowding out. Bekkers and Wiepking (2011) describe that "altruistic motivation (in the economic sense) would lead individuals who learn about an increase in contribution by others ... to reduce their own contribution [...]. This is called a 'crowding out' effect" (p. 936). The "crowding out" effect is contentious among scholars. Some studies have found no significant crowding out effects. For example, Brooks (2003) found that increased government support was correlated with higher numbers of donors, but with lower average private contributions. The perceived imbalance between community colleges and four-year institutions is negligible—the "crowding out" effect can happen to both types of institutions, and on different scales. The size of the campaign and amount of government resources and active donors affects the concept of "impure altruists" (Bekkers & Wiepking, 2011).

Reputation and Psychological Benefits. Reputation is important to philanthropists. Failure to give could damage an individual's reputation in his/her community (Bekkers & Wiepking, 2011; Drezner, 2011). Institutions must consider how they'll recognize donors. People want to feel connected to the institution, and are likely to donate if recognized appropriately (*cf.* Elliott, 2006).

When donors feel they're helping, the likelihood of future donations increases. Philanthropic events are crucial for increasing future giving (Elliott, 2006). Institutions of higher learning strive to enhance their public reputation. Alumni testimonials, campus experiences, coursework, and friendships made in college may conjure feelings of joy and development. Donors—such as alumni who may have had positive experiences while in college—choose to give because they hope future students have similar experiences. Reputation and the psychological benefits of giving are doubly important for philanthropists.

Values and Efficacy. Bekkers and Wiepking (2011) explain the role *values* play in philanthropy:

> Philanthropy is a means to reach a desired state of affairs that is closer to one's view of the "ideal" world. What that ideal world looks like depends on one's value system through giving, donors may wish to make the distribution of wealth and health more equal; they may wish to reduce poverty, empower women, safeguard human rights, to protect animals, wildlife or the ozone layer. Donors may also have objectives that are partisan or even terrorist. (p. 941)

Reasons for giving are personal and unique. The gift reflects the values of the donor(s) and therefore could be controversial. *Efficacy* is the "[donor's] perception ... that their contribution makes a difference to the cause they are supporting" (Bekkers & Wiepking, 2011, p. 942). Both mechanisms—values and efficacy—are vital to philanthropy within higher education because value decisions mark the types of gifts given and where gifts will reside (*cf.* Drezner, 2011).

More research is needed on what motivates donors to give. As earlier mentioned, state appropriations are declining, and private monies are becoming essential for meeting the changing needs of college students.

Yet, another imbalance between types of higher education institutions exists: private institutions have been excelling at gift solicitation since their inception, while public universities are catching up. Resources are vital to the success of any campaign or individual gift. Community colleges, often serving student populations with the greatest need, are languishing behind their four-year peers. Additionally, rural needs don't differ as much as most would believe compared to urban needs (e.g., poverty, drugs, teen pregnancy, etc.).

* * *

In the end, who benefits in higher education from a robust philanthropic environment? Just like at the Enrollment Management Conference at USC, I don't have clear answers, but I do have more questions that will guide my doctoral research.

The institution ultimately benefits; however, the administration, local government, and the donor also benefit. The benefits of giving can be felt both in infrastructure and psychological health. When things aren't going well, philanthropic efforts can be like *tapping a dry well*.

NOTE

[1] The Carnegie Classification of Institutions of Higher Education is a framework for classifying colleges and universities in the United States.

REFERENCES

Bekkers, R., & Wiepking, P. (2011). A literature review of empirical studies of philanthropy: Eight mechanisms that drive charitable giving. *Nonprofit and Voluntary Sector Quarterly*, *40*(5), 924–973. Retrieved from http://dx.doi.org/10.1177/0899764010380927

Brooks, A. C. (2003). Do government subsidies to non-profits crowd out donations or donors? *Public Finance Review*, *31*(2), 166–179. Retrieved from http://dx.doi.org/10.1177/1091142102250328

Cohen, A. M., Brawer, F. B., & Kisker, C. B. (2013). *The American community college* (6th ed.). San Francisco, CA: Jossey-Bass.

Drezner, N. D. (2011). Philanthropy and fundraising in American higher education (Special issue), *ASHE Higher Education Report, 37*(2), 1–155.

Drezner, N. D. (Eds.). (2013). *Expanding the donor base in higher education: Engaging non-traditional donors.* New York, NY: Routledge.

Elliott, D. (2006). *The kindness of strangers: Philanthropy and higher education.* Lanham, MD: Rowman & Littlefield.

Foderaro, L. W. (2011, January 16). Amid cuts, public colleges step up appeals to alumni. *The New York Times*, A1. Retrieved July 24, 2014, from http://www.nytimes.com/2011/01/16/education/16college.html/?pagewanted=all&_r=0

Goldrick-Rab, S., & Kendall, N. (2014). Redefining college affordability: Securing America's future with a free two-year college option. *The Education Optimists*. Retrieved July 23, 2014, fromhttp://www.theeduoptimists.com/category/publication

Hall, P. D. (1992). Teaching and research on philanthropy, voluntarism, and non-profit organizations: A case study of academic innovation. *Teachers College Record, 93*(3), 403–436. Retrieved July 17, 2014, from http://www.hks.harvard.edu/fs/phall/Teachers_College_Record1.pdf

MICHAEL E. JENNINGS

12. AFTER THE LOVE IS GONE

A Coda on the Importance of Critical Storytelling
in Uncritical Times

In a fundamental sense, telling stories is the quintessential human activity (Sandelowski, 1991). Telling stories shapes our existence vis-à-vis the world around us, and helps us sort through all of the complexities that it embodies (Bruner, 1990). Particularly for PK–12 classroom teachers and for college professors, storytelling serves as a means for connecting with colleagues and understanding our experiences in the classroom and on our campuses (Shank, 2006). Forging these connections and exploring the experiences that stem from them is especially important in the context of current neoliberal reform efforts. These efforts de-emphasize teacher and student autonomy while emphasizing accountability as a central feature of a market driven educational policy (Hursh, 2007). Such policies emphasize the role of teachers as technocrats who work towards the goal of increasing global effectiveness at all cost.

Part of this turn towards training teachers as technocrats is a move away from narrative ways of knowing that emphasize love, connectedness, and understanding between teachers and students. But what happens when the love is gone, the connections are lost, and previous understandings begin to fade? With these changes we see the rise of neoliberal educational policies that have emphasized a need for increased surveillance, discipline, and hyper-rationality both in PK–12 schools and on university campuses. The telling of stories challenges these hegemonic forces by helping teachers and teacher education candidates claim both agency and humanity through redirecting their gaze away from student surveillance and towards an understanding of the institutional structures that shape education in our society (Raible & Irizarry, 2010).

An important challenge for those who study the Cultural Foundations of Education is the ability to offer sustained critique of educational structures, practices, and policies that are centered on formal schooling while connecting these entities with larger societal structures that influence how knowledge

N. D. Hartlep & B. O. Hensley (Eds.), Critical Storytelling in Uncritical Times, 93–96.

is created and transmitted. *Critical Storytelling in Uncritical Times* rises to this challenge by chronicling the experience of students and faculty in a university class that challenged them to reflect on their personal experiences in creating a pedagogy best described as "students as curriculum" (Schubert & Schultz, 2015).

This pedagogy encourages both the students and the teacher to become active participants in a narrative tradition of storytelling that is transformative and interconnected in ways that reflect what Freire (1986) described as an act of "profound love" (p. 77). This love forms the basis of a pedagogy where love and dialogue are united in the context of narrative as a means to enhance learning.

Cho (2009) describes the profound possibilities of empowerment that are inherent in the unification of love and pedagogy in his psychoanalytic theory of education. He states that

> …love has the power to inspire students to seek after knowledge, love can unite the teacher and student in the quest for knowledge, and the love of learning can even empower students to challenge knowledge thereby pushing its limits.(p. 79)

By encouraging the idea of "self" as the focus of the curriculum, Hartlep and Hensley (2015) have advanced the notion of democratizing education in a way that respects the lived experiences of students while advancing the scholarship on storytelling in education. They have also put into practice a model that emphasizes speaking truth to power by utilizing narratives of teachers and students within a context of both love and knowledge. In doing this, the collective stories told in *Critical Storytelling in Uncritical Times* challenge the master narratives that sustain the established *status quo* in American education. To address these master narratives, Hartlep and Hensley (2015) have worked with their students to create a set of counternarratives that challenge the hegemonic structure of educational policies that define learning in terms of its ability to enhance American competitiveness in the global marketplace

The act of producing these counternarratives clearly demonstrates several reasons why students and professors should mutually engage one another in the writing process. First is the mutual understanding that comes via the writing process. This understanding helps both the student and the professor to understand the ideas and experiences of each other in mutually important and respectful ways. Second, it offers an opportunity for faculty to mentor students in the art of writing and research. This is especially important because faculty who work in teacher education programs frequently lament their students' lack of writing skills (Street, 2003) and their lack of knowledge about the process of research (Freeman, 1996). Acquiring these skills is an important and necessary part of the profession. Lastly, writing with students creates an excellent opportunity for faculty to engage them in the process of knowledge production (Zajano & Edelsberg, 1993). Participating in knowledge construction is of prime importance not just for those students seeking to become researchers, but also for those students who want to enhance their professional knowledge and skills as teachers and administrators (Prestine, 1995; So, 2013).

In summary, *Critical Storytelling in Uncritical Times* is more than an examination of theories related to teacher education and "narrative inquiry" (Clandinin & Connelly, 2000). It's a call to arms that illuminates a path for teachers, students, and faculty to use the power of storytelling to address important issues surrounding the current state of schooling in our society. In undertaking this important work, Hartlep and Hensley (2015) have helped to re-invigorate the potential for learning and praxis that is so often missing in the current practice of teacher education.

REFERENCES

Bruner, J. (1990). *Acts of meaning*. Cambridge, MA: Harvard University Press.
Clandinin, D. J., & Connelly, F. M. (2000). *Narrative inquiry: Experience and story in qualitative research*. San Franscisco, CA: Jossey-Bass.
Cho, K. D. (2009). *Psychopedagogy: Freud, Lacan, and the psychoanalytic theory of education*. New York, NY: Palgrave Macmillan.
Freeman, D. (1996). Redefining the relationship between research and what teachers know. In K. M. Bailey & D. Nunan (Eds.), *Voices from the language classroom: Qualitative research in second language education* (pp. 88–115). New York, NY: Cambridge University Press.
Freire, P. (1986). *Pedagogy of the oppressed*. New York, NY: Continuum.
Hartlep, N. D., & Hensley, B. O. (Eds.). (2015). *Critical storytelling in uncritical times: Stories disclosed in a cultural foundations of education course*. Rotterdam, The Netherlands: Sense Publishers.
Hursch, D. (2007). Assessing no child left behind and the rise of neoliberal education policies. *American Educational Research Journal, 44*(3), 493–518. Retrieved from http://dx.doi.org/10.3102/0002831207306764
Prestine, N. A. (1995). A constructivist view of the knowledge base in educational administration. In R. Donmoyer, M. Imber, & J. J. Scheurich (Eds.), *The knowledge base in educational administration: Multiple perspectives* (pp. 267–284). Albany, NY: State University of New York.
Raible, J., & Irizarry, J. G. (2010). Redirecting the teacher's gaze: Teacher education, youth surveillance and the school-to-prison pipeline. *Teaching and Teacher Education, 26*(5), 1196–1203. Retrieved from http://dx.doi.org/10.1016/j.tate.2010.02.006

Sandelowski, M. (1991). Telling stories: Narrative approaches in qualitative research. *Image: The Journal of Nursing Scholarship*, *23*(3), 161–166. Retrieved from http://dx.doi.org/10.1111/j.1547-5069.1991.tb00662.x

Schubert, W. H., & Schultz, B. D. (2015). Students as curriculum. In M. F. He, B. D. Schultz, & W. H. Schubert (Eds.), *The Sage guide to curriculum in education* (pp. 233–240). Thousand Oaks, CA: Sage.

Shank, M. J. (2006). Teacher storytelling: A means for creating and learning within a collaborative space. *Teaching and Teacher Education*, *22*(6), 711–721. Retrieved from http://dx.doi.org/10.1016/j.tate.2006.03.002

So, K. (2013). Knowledge construction among teachers within a community based on inquiry s stance. *Teaching and Teacher Education*, *29*, 188–196. Retrieved from http://dx.doi.org/10.1016/j.tate.2012.10.005

Street, C. (2003). Pre-service teachers' attitudes about writing and learning to teach writing: Implications for teacher educators. *Teacher Education Quarterly*, *30*(3), 33–50.

Zajano, N. C., & Edelsberg, C. M. (1993). Living and writing the researcher-researched relationship. *International Journal of Qualitative Studies in Education*, *6*(2), 143–157. Retrieved from http://dx.doi.org/10.1080/0951839930060204

CONTRIBUTORS

BOOK EDITORS

Nicholas D. Hartlep is currently an Assistant Professor of Educational Foundations at Illinois State University. Prior to that, he was an Advanced Opportunity Program Fellow at the University of Wisconsin-Milwaukee, an "Urban 13" University, where he earned a Ph.D. in the Social Foundations of Urban Education and was named an "Outstanding Doctoral Student." Dr. Hartlep also has a Master of Science degree in K–12 Education and a Bachelor of Science degree in Teaching, both conferred by Winona State University. As a former public school teacher he has taught in Rochester, Minnesota and Milwaukee, Wisconsin as well as abroad in Quito, Ecuador. Dr. Hartlep's research interests include urban in-service teachers' dispositions, the impact neoliberalism is having on schools and society, the model minority stereotype of Asians, and transracial adoption. His interest in transracial adoption stems from the fact that he was adopted from Seoul, South Korea when he was approximately 16 months old. In 2011, Dr. Hartlep received a scholarship from the Global Overseas Adoptees' Link (GOA'L) that allowed him to return to Korea to see where he was born. He received the University Research Initiative (URI) Award in 2015 from Illinois State University. His scholarly books include *Going Public: Critical Race Theory & Issues of Social Justice* (2010), *The Model Minority Stereotype: Demystifying Asian American Success* (2013), *Unhooking from Whiteness: The Key to Dismantling Racism in the United States* (2013), *The Model Minority Stereotype Reader: Critical and Challenging Readings for the 21st Century* (2014), *Modern Societal Impacts of the Model Minority Stereotype* (2015), *The Assault on Communities of Color: Exploring the Realities of Race-Based Violence* (2015), and *Killing the Model Minority Stereotype: Asian American Counterstories and Complicity* (2015). You can follow his work on Twitter @nhartlep and at www.nicholashartlep.com

Brandon O. Hensley is currently an Adjunct Professor and Coordinator of Assessment at a small, private university in Illinois. He is a doctoral candidate in the Department of Educational Administration and Foundations at Illinois State University. Brandon received his Master of Arts in Communication Studies from Eastern Illinois University. His research interests include critical communication pedagogy, rhetorical/media criticism, intersectionality of

97

hegemonic social constructs, and the working conditions of adjunct educators in U.S. colleges and universities. Hensley has presented more than 30 papers at regional, national, and international conferences, and he currently serves as division F co-chair in the Mid-Western Educational Research Association (MWERA). His recent published work includes "How Far From Income Equity are Faculty in Four-Year, Non-Doctoral Universities?" published in *Journal of Academic Administration in Higher Education* and "It Takes More Than Public Speaking: A Leadership Analysis of *The King's Speech*" published in *The Journal of Organizational Learning and Leadership.* You can follow his work on Academia.edu and BePress.

COMMISSIONED COVER ARTIST

Tak Toyoshima is the creative director at the award-winning alternative newsweekly newspaper *DigBoston*. He is also the creator and illustrator of *Secret Asian Man*, a comic strip that started in 1999 that focuses on the divisive issues of race, gender, religion, politics, and anything else that causes us to be placed into identifiable groups.

CHAPTER AUTHORS

Saad Alahmari is a Ph.D. student majoring in Higher Education Administration at Illinois State University. He earned his M.B.A. from the University of Scranton. Saad worked as an HR supervisor at Marafiq, a utilities company. In 2013, he was granted to pursue his Ph.D. by the King Abdulla scholarships program. Saad chose to study Higher Education Administration in the United States because the United States has one of the best educational systems worldwide. He realized when he was in the Kingdom of Saudi Arabia (KSA) that the lack of universities was an issue with the huge number of young students in KSA. Therefore, he wants to use his master's in business and Ph.D. in higher education administration to help the new private schools, which are encouraged by the Saudi government.

Cyndy Alvarez is a third year doctoral student in the School Psychology program in the Psychology Department at Illinois State University. She received her Bachelor of Arts in Psychology from St. Mary's University in San Antonio, Texas. Cyndy is currently a clinician at The Autism Place (TAP) and a mental health consultant at Head Start. She previously participated as a mentor under the CONNECT Mentorship Program at Illinois State University.

She will be conducting research regarding college adjustment among ethnic minority students. She also has research interests in the developmental and mental health impacts among children with undocumented parents.

Derek M. Bolen is the Graduate Director and an Assistant Professor in the Department of Communication and Mass Media at Angelo State University. He teaches courses on relational communication, qualitative research, gender and sexuality, communication theory, communication pedagogy, and ethics in communication. His research has been published in journals such as *Cultural Studies ↔ Critical Methodologies, Communication Education, Communication Studies*, and *Western Journal of Communication*. He is the founder and director of the international *Doing Autoethnography* conference, an annual convention entering its fourth year.

Michael Cermak is a veteran educator with experiences at secondary schools, community colleges, and a university. He has served as faculty, high school principal, sponsored project director and dean. His research interests include equity issues around career and technical education.

Erik Dalmasso is currently the Associate Director of Client Strategy for Ruffalo-Cody, an enrollment management consulting group. He has served in a variety of admissions positions at several public and private Illinois institutions for over ten years. Erik holds a Master of Science in College Student Personnel Administration and a Bachelor of Science degree from Illinois State University. His research interest in rural post-secondary education and opportunity stems from his time as a student at Spoon River College, earning an Associate's degree directly after high school. Erik is preparing for the final phase of his doctoral program, and is excited to work on post-secondary opportunities for students in west-central Illinois.

Christopher Downing is currently the Executive Director of a Foundation for a local community college. He is in his second year of doctoral studies in the Educational Administration and Foundations higher education program in the College of Education at Illinois State University. He holds a Master of Arts in Public Administration from Northern Illinois University and a Bachelor of Arts in Speech Communication and Political Science from Augustana College. Christopher's career focus has been development and fundraising for social service agencies and community colleges.

Michael E. Jennings currently serves as an Associate Professor in the Department of Educational Leadership and Policy Studies and as an Associate Dean in the College of Education and Human Development at the University of Texas at San Antonio. His research focuses on cultural and racial diversity in education, critical race theory, and narrative/autobiography in educational context.

Jamie Neville is a third year doctoral student in the Educational Administration and Foundations higher education program in the College of Education at Illinois State University. He currently works in University Housing Services at Illinois State University, building communities and fostering leadership for undergraduate students. He is currently the Area Coordinator of Watterson Towers, the tallest residence hall in the nation. He frequently presents at regional and national conferences on various topics related to residence life. Jamie holds a Master of Arts in Leadership in Human Service Administration and a Bachelor of Science in Secondary Education, both from Bradley University.

Kathleen O'Brien is a second year doctoral student in Educational Administration and Foundations at Illinois State University. She previously taught in K–12 settings and also taught developmental reading at a community college. The focus of these experiences was critical literacy and culturally relevant pedagogy, which emerged from scholarship while earning a master's in reading. In her master's work, she conducted qualitative research on Ruby Payne's impact on teacher beliefs and practices, presenting this data at the AERA conference in 2007. She also was involved in a research project analyzing code-switching practices of students at a high-poverty high school in Peoria, Illinois and presented the findings at the Illinois Reading Council Conference in 2009. Kathleen holds a Master of Science in Criminal Justice Sciences, Reading, and a Bachelor of Science in Sociology and Education from Illinois State University. She is currently teaching Social Foundations of Education courses as part of her doctoral program.

Amanda Rohan is a second year doctoral student in the School Psychology program in the Psychology Department at Illinois State University. She received her Bachelors of Science degrees in Psychology and Family and Child Sciences from Florida State University. Prior to graduate school, she worked as a research assistant for the Florida Center for Reading Research on the Reading for Understanding project and Project BLOOM. During her first year of graduate school, she provided classroom assistance and social-emotional interventions during a pre-practicum experience at Head Start, and she continues to be a clinician at The Autism Program. She is a member of research teams at ISU that focus on early childhood Social Emotional Learning programs and the cognitive consequences of racial microaggressions. Amanda's research interests also include academic and behavioral interventions, early intervention, and alternative education systems.

Tuwana T. Wingfield is a fourth year doctoral student in the Educational Administration and Foundations higher education program in the College of Education at Illinois State University. She received her Bachelor of Arts in Sociology from Purdue University and her Artium Magister in Social Work from the University of Chicago, School of Social Service Administration and is a licensed clinical social worker in the State of Illinois. Her areas of interest are feminism, critical theory, culturally responsive education, social justice, identity development, mentoring, and research methods in education.

AUTHOR INDEX

SUBJECT INDEX